GATHER TOGETHER IN MY NAME

GATHER TOGETHER IN MY NAME

Maya Angelou

BANTAM BOOKS

New York   Toronto   London

Sydney   Auckland

RL 8, IL age 14 and up

GATHER TOGETHER IN MY NAME

A Bantam Book / published by arrangement with Random House, Inc.

PUBLISHING HISTORY

Random House edition published April 1974
Bantam mass market edition / May 1975
Bantam trade edition / June 1997

ISBN 0-553-37997-6

Published simultaneously in the United States and Canada

Bantam Books are published by Bantam Books, a division of Bantam Doubleday Dell Publishing Group, Inc. Its trademark, consisting of the words "Bantam Books" and the portrayal of a rooster, is Registered in U.S. Patent and Trademark Office and in other countries. Marca Registrada. Bantam Books, 1540 Broadway, New York, New York 10036.

PRINTED IN THE UNITED STATES OF AMERICA

10   9   8   7   6   5   4   3   2   1

This book is dedicated to my blood brother

BAILEY JOHNSON

and to the other real brothers who encouraged me
to be bodacious enough to invent my own life daily:

JAMES BALDWIN

KWESI BREW

DAVID DU BOIS

SAMUEL FLOYD

JOHN O. KILLENS

VAGABOND KING

LEO MAITLAND

VUSUMZI MAKE

JULIAN MAYFIELD

MAX ROACH

A special thanks to my friend
DOLLY MCPHERSON

IT was a "come as you are" party and "all y'all come." If you bring your own bottle, you'll be expected to share; if you don't it's all right, somebody will share with you. It was triumph and brotherhood. Everybody was a hero. Hadn't we all joined together to kick the hell out of *de Gruber*, and that fat Italian, and put that little rice-eating Tojo in his place?

Black men from the South who had held no tools more complicated than plows had learned to use lathes and borers and welding guns, and had brought in their quotas of war-making machines. Women who had only known maid's uniforms and mammy-made dresses donned the awkward men's pants and steel helmets, and made the ship-fitting sheds hum some buddy. Even the children had collected paper, and at the advice of elders who remembered World War I, balled the tin foil from cigarettes and chewing gum into balls as big as your head. Oh, it was a time.

Soldiers and sailors, and the few black Marines fresh from having buried death on a sandy South Pacific beach, stood around looking proud out of war-wise eyes.

Black-marketeers had sped around a million furtive corners trying to keep the community supplied with sugar, cigarettes, rationing stamps and butter. Prostitutes didn't even
take the time to remove their seventy-five dollar shoes when
they turned twenty-dollar tricks. Everyone was a part of the
war effort.

And at last it had paid off in spades. We had won. Pimps
got out of their polished cars and walked the streets of
San Francisco only a little uneasy at the unusual exercise.
Gamblers, ignoring their sensitive fingers, shook hands
with shoeshine boys. Pulpits rang with the "I told you so"
of ministers who knew that God was on the side of right
and He would not see the righteous forsaken, nor their
young beg bread. Beauticians spoke to the shipyard workers,
who in turn spoke to the easy ladies. And everybody had soft
little preparation-to-smile smiles on their faces.

I thought if war did not include killing, I'd like to see one
every year. Something like a festival.

All the sacrifices had won us victory and now the good
times were coming. Obviously, if we earned more than
rationing would allow us to spend during wartime, things
were really going to look up when restrictions were removed.

There was no need to discuss racial prejudice. Hadn't we
all, black and white, just snatched the remaining Jews from
the hell of concentration camps? Race prejudice was dead. A
mistake made by a young country. Something to be forgiven
as an unpleasant act committed by an intoxicated friend.

During the crisis, black people had often made more
money in a month then they had seen in their whole lives.
Black men did not leave their wives, driven away by an
inability to provide for their families. They rode in public
transport on a first-come/first-seated basis. And more times

than not were called Mister/Missus at their jobs or by sales clerks.

Two months after V-Day, war plants began to shut down, to cut back, to lay off employees. Some workers were offered tickets back to their Southern homes. Back to the mules they had left tied to the tree on ole Mistah Doo hickup farm. No good. Their expanded understanding could never again be accordioned into these narrow confines. They were free or at least nearer to freedom than ever before and they would not go back.

Those military heroes of a few months earlier, who were discharged from the Army in the city which knows how, began to be seen hanging on the ghetto corners like forgotten laundry left on a backyard fence. Their once starched khaki uniforms were gradually bastardized. An ETO jacket, plus medals, minus stripes, was worn with out-of-fashion zoot pants. The trim army pants, creases trained in symmetry, were topped by loud, color-crazed Hawaiian shirts. The shoes remained. Only the shoes. The Army had made those shoes to last. And dammit, they did.

Thus we lived through a major war. The question in the ghettos was, Can we make it through a minor peace?

I was seventeen, very old, embarrassingly young, with a son of two months, and I still lived with my mother and stepfather.

They offered me a chance to leave my baby with them and return to school. I refused. First, I reasoned with the righteous seriousness of youth, I was not Daddy Clidell Jackson's blood daughter and my child was his grandchild only as long as the union between Daddy and Mother held fast, and by then I had seen many weak links in their chain of marriage. Second, I considered that although I was Mother's child, she had left me with others until I was thirteen and why should she feel more responsibility for my child than she had felt for her own. Those were the pieces that made up the skin of my refusal, but the core was more painful, more solid, truer. A textured guilt was my familiar, my bedmate to whom I had turned my back. My daily companion whose hand I would not hold. The Christian teaching dinned into my ears in the small town in Arkansas would not be quieted by the big-city noise.

My son had no father—so what did that make me? According to the Book, bastards were not to be allowed into the congregation of the righteous. There it was. I would get a job, and a room of my own, and take my beautiful son out into the world. I thought I might even move to another town and change our names.

During the months when I was tussled with my future and that of my son, the big house we lived in began to die. Suddenly jobless roomers, who lined their solemn trunks with memories before they packed in folds of disappointment, left San Francisco for Los Angeles, Chicago, Detroit, where "they say" jobs were begging for workers. The loud slams of the front doors were heard more seldom, and the upstairs kitchen, where the roomers exercised their cooking privileges, gave fewer and fewer of the exotic aromas which used to send me running to our kitchen for snacks.

The gamblers and prostitutes, black-marketeers and boosters, all those suckerfish who had gotten fat living on the underbelly of the war, were the last to feel the pinch. They had accumulated large masses of money, which never went into a bank, but circulated among their tribe like promiscuous women, and by the nature of their professions, they were accustomed to the infidelity of Lady Luck and the capriciousness of life. I was sorry to see the dancers go—those glamorous women, only slightly older than I, who wore pounds of Max Factor No. 31, false eyelashes and talked out of the sides of their mouths, their voices sliding around cigarettes which forever dangled from their lips. They had often practiced their routines in the downstairs kitchen. The B.S. Chorus. Time steps, slides, flashes and breaks, smoking all the time. I was fairly certain that in order to be a chorus dancer, one would have to smoke.

By no amount of agile exercising of a wishful imagination could my mother have been called lenient. Generous she was; indulgent, never. Kind, yes; permissive, never. In her world, people she accepted paddled their own canoes, pulled their own weight, put their own shoulders to their own plows and pushed like hell, and here I was in her house, refusing to go back to school. Not giving a thought to marriage (admittedly, no one asked me) and working at nothing. At no time did she advise me to seek work. At least not in words. But the strain of her nights at the pinochle table, the responsibility of the huge sums which were kept in the bedroom closet, wore on her already short temper.

In earlier, freer days I might have simply noted and recorded her grumpiness, but now my guilt, which I carried around like a raw egg, fed my paranoia, and I became sure that I was a nuisance. When my baby cried I rushed to change him, feed him, coddle him, to in fact shut him up. My youth and shuddering self-doubt made me unfair to that vital woman.

She took great joy in her beautiful grandchild, and as with most egocentric people, saw his every virtue as a mirror for her own. He had pretty hands ... "Well, look at mine." His feet were absolutely straight with high insteps; so were hers. She was not annoyed with me; she was playing the hand life had dealt her as she had always done. And she played it masterfully.

The mixture of arrogance and insecurity is as volatile as the much-touted alcohol and gasoline. The difference is that with the former there is a long internal burning usually terminating in self-destroying implosion.

I would quit the house, take a job and show the whole world (my son's father) that I was equal to my pride and greater than my pretensions.

CHAPTER 1

───────── ✐ ─────────

I WAS mortified. A silly white woman who probably counted on her toes looked me in the face and said I had not passed. The examination had been constructed by morons for idiots. Of course I breezed through without thinking much about it.

REARRANGE THESE LETTERS: ACT-ART-AST

Okay. CAT. RAT. SAT. Now what?

She stood behind her make-up and coiffed hair and manicured nails and dresser-drawers of scented angora sweaters and years of white ignorance and said that I had not passed.

"The telephone company spends thousands of dollars training operators. We simply cannot risk employing anyone who made the marks you made. I'm sorry."

She was sorry? I was stunned. In a stupor I considered that maybe my outsized intellectual conceit had led me to take the test for granted. And maybe I deserved this high-handed witch's remarks.

"May I take it again?" That was painful to ask.

"No, I'm sorry." If she said she was sorry one more time, I was going to take her by her sorry shoulders and shake a job out of her.

"There is an opening, though"—she might have sensed my unspoken threat—"for a bus girl in the cafeteria."

"What does a bus girl do?" I wasn't sure I could do it.

"The boy in the kitchen will tell you."

After I filled out forms and was found uninfected by a doctor, I reported to the cafeteria. There the boy, who was a grandfather, informed me, "Collect the dishes, wipe the tables, make sure the salt and pepper shakers are clean, and here's your uniform."

The coarse white dress and apron had been starched with concrete and was too long. I stood at the side of the room, the dress hem scratching my calves, waiting for the tables to clear. Many of the trainee operators had been my classmates. Now they stood over laden tables waiting for me or one of the other dumb bus girls to remove the used dishes so that they could set down their trays.

I lasted at the job a week, and so hated the salary that I spent it all the afternoon I quit.

CHAPTER 2

———— ⟐ ————

"CAN you cook Creole?"

I looked at the woman and gave her a lie as soft as melting butter. "Yes, of course. That's all I know how to cook."

The Creole Café had a cardboard sign in the window which bragged: COOK WANTED. SEVENTY-FIVE DOLLARS A WEEK. As soon as I saw it I knew I could cook Creole, whatever that was.

Desperation to find help must have blinded the proprietress to my age or perhaps it was the fact that I was nearly six feet and had an attitude which belied my seventeen years. She didn't question me about recipes and menus, but her long brown face did trail down in wrinkles, and doubt hung on the edges of her questions.

"Can you start on Monday?"

"I'll be glad to."

"You know it's six days a week. We're closed on Sunday."

"That's fine with me. I like to go to church on Sunday."

It's awful to think that the devil gave me that lie, but it came unexpectedly and worked like dollar bills. Suspicion and doubt raced from her face, and she smiled. Her teeth were all the same size, a small white picket fence semicircled in her mouth.

"Well, I know we're going to get along. You a good Christian. I like that. Yes, ma'am, I sure do."

My need for a job caught and held the denial.

"What time on Monday?" Bless the Lord!

"You get here at five."

Five in the morning. Those mean streets before the thugs had gone to sleep, pillowing on someone else's dreams. Before the streetcars began to rattle, their lighted insides like exclusive houses in the fog. Five!

"All right, I'll be here at five, Monday morning."

"You'll cook the dinners and put them on the steam table. You don't have to do short orders. I do that."

Mrs. Dupree was a short plump woman of about fifty. Her hair was naturally straight and heavy. Probably Cajun Indian, African and white, and naturally, Negro.

"And what's your name?"

"Rita." Marguerite was too solemn, and Maya too rich-sounding. "Rita" sounded like dark flashing eyes, hot peppers and Creole evenings with strummed guitars. "Rita Johnson."

"That's a right nice name." Then, like some people do to show their sense of familiarity, she immediately narrowed the name down. "I'll call you Reet. Okay?"

Okay, of course. I had a job. Seventy-five dollars a week. So I was Reet. Reet, poteet and gone. All Reet. Now all I had to do was learn to cook.

CHAPTER 3

―――――――――― ∼≫ ――――――――――

I ASKED old Papa Ford to teach me how to cook. He had been a grown man when the twentieth century was born, and left a large family of brothers and sisters in Terre Haute, Indiana (always called the East Coast), to find what the world had in store for a "good-looking colored boy with no education in his head, but a pile of larceny in his heart." He traveled with circuses "shoveling elephant shit." He then shot dice in freight trains and played koch in back rooms and shanties all over the Northern states.

"I never went down to Hang'em High. Them crackers would have killed me. Pretty as I was, white women was always following me. The white boys never could stand a pretty nigger."

By 1943, when I first saw him, his good looks were as delicate as an old man's memory, and disappointment rode his face bareback. His hands had gone. Those gambler's fingers had thickened during the Depression, and his only straight job, carpenting, had further toughened his "money-makers." Mother rescued him from a job as a sweeper in a pinochle parlor and brought him home to live with us.

He sorted and counted the linen when the laundry truck picked it up and returned it, then grudgingly handed out fresh sheets to the roomers. He cooked massive and delicious dinners when Mother was busy, and he sat in the tall-ceilinged kitchen drinking coffee by the pots.

Papa Ford loved my mother (as did nearly everyone) with a childlike devotion. He went so far as to control his profanity when she was around, knowing she couldn't abide cursing unless she was the curser.

"Why the sheeit do you want to work in a goddam kitchen?"

"Papa, the job pays seventy-five dollars a week."

"Busting some goddam suds." Disgust wrinkled his face.

"Papa, I'll be cooking and not washing dishes."

"Colored women been cooking so long, thought you'd be tired of it by now."

"If you'll just tell me—"

"Got all that education. How come you don't get a goddam job where you can go to work looking like something?"

I tried another tack. "I probably couldn't learn to cook Creole food, anyway. It's too complicated."

"Sheeit. Ain't nothing but onions, green peppers and garlic. Put that in everything and you got Creole food. You know how to cook rice, don't you?"

"Yes." I could cook it till each grain stood separately.

"That's all, then. Them geechees can't live without swamp seed." He cackled at his joke, then recalled a frown. "Still don't like you working as a goddam cook. Get married, then you don't have to cook for nobody but your own family. Sheeit."

CHAPTER 4

THE Creole Café steamed with onion vapor, garlic mists, tomato fogs and green-pepper sprays. I cooked and sweated among the cloying odors and loved being there. Finally I had the authority I had always longed for. Mrs. Dupree chose the daily menu, and left a note on the steam table informing me of her gastronomic decisions. But, I, Rita, the chef, decided how much garlic went into the baked short rib à la Creole, how many bay leaves would flavor the steamed Shreveport tripe. For over a month I was embroiled in the mysteries of the kitchen with the expectancy of an alchemist about to discover the secret properties of gold.

A leathered old white woman, whom Mother found, took care of my baby while I worked. I had been rather reluctant to leave him in her charge, but Mother reminded me that she tended her white, black and Filipino children equally well. I reasoned that her great age had shoved her beyond the pale of any racial differences. Certainly anyone who lived that long had to spend any unused moments thinking about death and the life to come. She simply couldn't afford the precious time to think of prejudices. The greatest compensation for youth's illness is the utter ignorance of the seriousness of the affliction.

Only after the mystery was worn down to a layer of commonness did I begin to notice the customers. They consisted largely of light-skinned, slick-haired Creoles from Louisiana, who spoke a French patois only a little less complicated than the contents of my pots and equally spicy. I thought it fitting and not at all unusual that they enjoyed my cooking. I was following Papa Ford's instructions loosely and adding artistic touches of my own.

Our customers never ate, paid and left. They sat on the long backless stools and exchanged gossip or shared the patient philosophy of the black South.

"Take it easy, Greasy, you got a long way to slide."

With the tolerance of ages they gave and accepted advice.

"Take it easy, but take it."

One large ruddy man, whose name I never knew, allowed his elbows to support him at the twelve-stool counter, and told tales of the San Francisco waterfront: "They got wharf rats who fight a man flat-footed."

"No?" A voice wanted to believe.

"Saw one of those suckers the other night backed a cracker up 'gainst a cargo crate. Hadn't been for me and two other guys, colored guys"—naturally—"he'd of run down his throat and walked on his liver."

Near the steam counter, the soft sounds of black talk, the sharp reports of laughter, and the shuffling feet on tiled floors mixed themselves in odorous vapors and I was content.

CHAPTER 5

I HAD rented a room (with cooking privileges) in a tall, imposing San Francisco Victorian and had bought my first furniture and a white chenille bedspread. God, but it looked like a field of tiny snow roses. I had a beautiful child, who laughed to see me, a job that I did well, a baby-sitter whom I trusted, and I was young and crazy as a road lizard. Surely this was making it.

One foggy evening on my day off, I had picked up my son and was carrying him home along the familiar streets with the casual ease of an old mother. He snoozed in the angle of my arm, and I thought of dinner, and the radio and a night of reading. Two ex-schoolmates came up the hill toward me. They were of that rare breed, black born San Franciscans. I, cushioned in my maturity, didn't think to further arm myself. I had the arrowproof vest of adult confidence, so I let them approach—easy.

"Let us look at the baby . . . I hear he's cute." She was fat with small covetous eyes and was known for having a tiny but pugnacious wit. Her friend, Lily, even as a teen-ager, was old beyond knowing and bored beyond wisdom.

"Yes. They say you made a pretty baby."

I lifted the flap of light blanket from my son's face and shifted myself so that they might see my glory.

"My God, you did that?" The fat one's face broke open into a wounded grin.

Her somber friend intoned, "Jesus, he looks like he's white. He could pass." Her word floated into my air on admiration and wonder. I shriveled that she could say such a terrible thing about my baby, but I had no nerve to cover my prize and walk away. I stood dumfounded, founded in dumbness.

The short one laughed a crackly laugh and pushed the point between my ribs. "He's got a little nose and thin lips." Her surprise was maddening. "As long as you live and troubles rise, you ought to pay the man for giving you that baby, huh. A crow gives birth to a dove. The bird kingdom must be petrified."

There's a point in fury when one becomes abject. Motionless. I froze, as Lot's wife must have done, having caught a last glimpse of concentrated evil.

"And what did you name him? 'Thank God A-mighty'?"

I could have laid him down there, bunting and all, and left him for someone who had more grace, more style and beauty. My own pride of control would not allow me to show the girls what I was feeling, so I covered my baby and headed home. No good-byes—I left them as if I were planning to walk off the edge of the world. In my room I lay my five months of belongingness on the chenilled bed and sat beside him to look over his perfection. His little head was exactly round and the soft hair curled up in black ripples. His arms and legs were plump marvels, and his torso as straight as a look between lovers. But it was his face with which I had to do.

Admittedly, the lips were thin and traced themselves sparely under a small nose. But he was a baby, and as he grew, these abnormalities would flesh out, become real, imitate the regularity of my features. His eyes, even closed, slanted up toward his throbbing temples. He looked like a baby Buddha. And then I examined his hairline. It followed mine in every detail. And that would not grow away or change, and it proved that he was undeniably mine.

CHAPTER 6

———— ✐ ————

BUTTER-COLORED, honey-brown, lemon- and olive-skinned. Chocolate and plum-blue, peaches-and-cream. Cream. Nutmeg. Cinnamon. I wondered why my people described our colors in terms of something good to eat. Then God's prettiest man became a customer at my restaurant.

He sat beside the light-skinned Creoles, and they thinned and paled and disappeared. His dark-brown skin glistened, and the reflected light made it hard to look into my mysterious pots. His voice to the waitress was a thumb poking in my armpits. I hated his being there because his presence made me jittery, but I loathed his leaving and could hardly bear waiting for him to return.

The waitress and Mrs. Dupree called him "Curly," but I thought whoever named him little used their imagination. When he opened the steamy door to the restaurant, surely it was the second coming of Christ.

His table manners pleased me. He ate daintily and slowly as if he cared what he put in his mouth. He smiled at me, but the nervous grimaces I gave him in return couldn't even loosely be called smiles. He was friendly with the customers, the waitress and me, since he always came alone. I wondered why he didn't have girl friends. Any woman would give a pretty to go out with him or rush to sit and talk to him. I never thought he would find me interesting, and if he did, it would be just to tease me.

"Reet." There it was. I acted as if I hadn't heard him.

"Reet. You hear me. Come here."

I have seen bitch dogs in heat sidle sinuously along the ground, tempting, luring. I would like to be able to say I went to him so naturally. Unfortunately not. I draped myself in studied indifference and inched out my voice in disdainful measures.

"Were you speaking to me?"

"Come here, I won't bite." Looking down upon his request, I conceded. If he was beautiful from a distance, up close he was perfection. His eyes were deep-black and slow-lidded. His upper lip arched and fell over white teeth held together in the middle by the merest hint of yellow gold.

"How long you been knowing to cook like that?"

"All my life." I could hardly make the lie leave my tongue.

"You married?"

"No."

"You be careful, somebody's gonna come here and kidnap you."

"Thank you." Why didn't he? Of course he would have had to knock me down, bind and gag me, but I would have liked nothing better.

"You want a soda?"

"No thanks." I turned and went back to the steam table, sweat nibbling above my top lip and under my arms. I wished him away but could feel his gaze on my back. I had spent so many years being people other than myself that I continued to stir and mix, raise and lower burners as if every nerve in my body were not attached to the third stool of the lunch counter.

The door opened and closed and I turned to watch his retreating back, only to find that another customer had left. Automatically I looked for him and met his eyes, solemn on me. I burned at giving myself away.

He nodded me over.

"What time you get off?"

"One o'clock."

"Want me to take you home?"

"I usually go out to see my baby."

"You've got a baby? Somebody must of give it to you for Christmas. A doll baby. How old are you?"

"Nineteen." Sometimes I was twenty, or eighteen. It depended on my mood.

"Nineteen going on seventeen." His smile held no ridicule. Just a smidgen of indulgence.

"Okay. I'll take you to see your baby."

HE drove his 1941 Pontiac without seeming to think about it. I sat in the corner pushed against the door trying desperately not to watch him.

"Where's the baby's daddy?"

"I don't know."

"He wouldn't marry you, huh?" His voice hardened in the question.

"I didn't want to marry him." Partly true.

"Well, he's a low-down bastard in my book and needs his ass kicked." I began to love him at that moment.

I shifted to look at him. My avenging angel. Mother and my brother had been so busy being positive and supportive, neither had given any thought to the possibility that I might want revenge. I don't think I had even thought about it before. Now anger was an injection that flooded my body, making me warm and excited.

That's true, he was a low-life bastard. He should have given me a chance to refuse his proposal. Out of my head and into forgetfulness went the memory that I had wilfully initiated my one sexual tryst. My personal reasons and aggressive tactics were conveniently obliterated. Self-pity in its early stage is as snug as a feather mattress. Only when it hardens does it become uncomfortable.

Curly stood in the center of the baby-sitter's living room and said all the mother-liking things: "Sure is a fine baby . . . Looks just like you . . . He's gonna be a big one . . . Check those feet."

Back in the car it never occurred to me to put up resistance when he said we were going to his hotel. I wanted to do what he wanted, so I sat quiet.

As we passed through the hotel lobby, I felt the first stirring of reluctance. Now, wait a minute. What was I doing here? What did he think I was? He hadn't even said he loved me. Where was the soft music that should be playing as he kissed my ear lobe?

He sensed the hesitation and took my hand to guide me down the carpeted hallway. His touch and confidence rushed my doubts. Obviously I couldn't stop now.

"Make yourself comfortable."

He removed his coat and I sat quickly in the one large chair. On the dresser, amid cards and toiletries, stood a bottle of whiskey.

"May I have a drink?" I had never drunk anything stronger than Dubonnet.

"No. I don't think so. But I'll have one." He poured the liquor into a glass he took down from above the face bowl. Water sloshed around and he gulped it down. Then in a moment he stood over me. I wanted to look up at him but my head refused.

"Come here, Reet. Get up." I wanted to, but my muscles had atrophied. I didn't want him to think of me as a dick teaser. A cheat. But my body wouldn't obey.

He bent and took both hands and pulled me upright. He enclosed me in his arms.

"You nearly 'bout as tall as me. I like tall girls." Then he kissed me, softly. And slowly. When he stopped, my body had gone its own way. My heart raced and my knees were locked. I was embarrassed at my trembling.

"Come over to the bed." He patiently pulled me away from the chair.

We both sat on the bed and I could hardly see him, although he was a breath away. He held my face in his large dark hands.

"I know you're scared. That's natural. You're young. But we're going to have a party. Just think of it like that. We're having a love party."

My previous brushes with sex had been just that. Brushes. One violent. The other indifferent, and now I found myself in the hands and arms of a tender man.

He stroked and talked. He kissed me until my ears rang, and he made me laugh. He interrupted his passion to make some small joke, and the second I responded he resumed lovemaking.

I lay crying in his arms, after.

"You happy?" The gold in his mouth glinted like a little star.

I was so happy that the next day I went to a jewelers and bought him an onyx ring with a diamond chip. I charged it to my stepfather's account.

CHAPTER 7

———— ✒ ————

LOVE was what I had been waiting for. I had done grown-up things out of childish ignorance or juvenile bravado, but now I began to mature. I became pleased with my body because it gave me such pleasure. I shopped for myself carefully for the first time. Searching painstakingly for just the right clothes instead of buying the first thing off the rack. Unfortunately my taste was as new as my interest. Once when Curly was to take me out to dinner, I bought a smart yellow crepe dress with black roses, black baby-doll shoes, whose straps sank a full inch into my ankles, and an unflattering wide coolie hat with veil. I pinned a small cluster of yellow rose buds on my bosom and was ready for the fray.

He only asked me to remove the corsage.

Curly had said at the beginning of our affair that he had a girl who worked in a San Diego shipyard and her job would be up soon. Then they'd go back to New Orleans and get married. I hastily stored the information in that inaccessible region of the mind where one puts the memory of pain and other unpleasantries. For the while it needn't bother me, and it didn't.

He was getting out of the Navy and only had a couple of months before all his papers would be cleared. Southern upbringing and the terror of war made him seem much older than his thirty-one years.

We took my son for long walks through parks; when people complimented us on our child, he played the proud papa and accepted. At playland on the beach we rode the Ferris wheel and loop-the-loop and gooed ourselves with salt-water taffy. Late afternoons we took the baby back to the sitter and then went to his hotel and one more, or two more, or three more love parties. I never wanted it to end. I bought things for him. A watch (he already had one), a sports coat (too small), another ring, and paid for them myself. I couldn't hear his protestations. I wasn't buying things. I was buying time.

One day after work he took me to the sitter's. He sat and held the baby. His silence should have told me something. Maybe it did, but again I didn't want to know. We left in a quiet mood. He only said, "I want me a boy like that. Just like that."

Since we weren't heading for the hotel, I asked where we were going.

"I'm taking you to your house."

"Why?"

No answer.

He found a parking space a half-block away. The street-lights were just coming on and a soft fog dimmed the world. He reached in the back seat and took out two large boxes. He handed them to me and said, "Give me a kiss."

I tried to laugh, to pretend that the kiss was payment for the gifts, but the laugh lied. He kissed me lightly and looked at me long.

"Reet. My girl friend is here and I'll be checking out of the hotel tonight."

I didn't cry because I couldn't think.

"You're going to make some man a wonderful wife. I mean it. These things are for you and the baby. I hate to say good-bye, but I gotta."

He probably said more, but all I remember is walking from the car to my front door. Trying for my life's sake to control the angry lurchings of my stomach. Trying to walk upright carrying the awkward boxes. I had to set down the boxes to find the door key, and habit fitted it into the lock. I entered the hall without hearing him start the car.

Because he had not lied, I was forbidden anger. Because he had patiently and tenderly taught me love, I could not use hate to ease the pain. I had to bear it.

I am certain, with the passage of time, that he loved me. Maybe for the loveless waif I was. Maybe he felt pity for the young mother and fatherless child, and so decided to give us what we both needed for two months. I don't know. I'm only certain that for some reason he loved me and that he was a good man.

The loss of young first love is so painful that it borders on the ludicrous.

I even embarrassed myself. Weeks after Charles left, I stumbled around San Francisco operating in the familiar. The lovely city disappeared in my fog. Nothing I did to food made it interesting to me. Music became a particular aggravation, for every emotional lyric had obviously been written for me alone.

Gonna take a sentimental journey
gonna set my heart at ease . . .

CHARLES had taken that journey and left me all alone. I was one emotional runny sore. To be buffeted about emotionally was not new, only the intensity and reason were. The new pain and discomfort was physical. My body had been awakened and fed, and suddenly I discovered I had a ravenous appetite. My natural reticence and habit of restraint prevented me from seeking other satisfaction even if it could be found.

I began to lose weight, which, with my height and thinness, I could ill afford to do. The burst of energy which had propelled me into beauty salons and dress shops was now as absent as my gone lover. I longed and pined, sighed and yearned, cried and generally slouched around feeling dismal and bereaved. By eighteen I managed to look run down if not actually run over.

My brother Bailey again was my savior, a role he fulfilled most of my early years.

He returned to the city after some months on an ammunition ship, and came to the restaurant to see me.

"My. What the hell's happened to you?" The way I looked seemed to anger rather than worry him. I introduced him to my employer. She said, "Your brother. He awful little, ain't he? I mean, to be your brother?"

Bailey thanked her smoothly, allowing just the tail of his sarcasm to flick in her face. She never noticed.

"I said, what's the matter with you? Have you been sick?" I held in the tears that wanted to pour into my brother's hands.

"No. I'm okay."

I thought at the time that it was noble to bear the ills one had silently. But not so silently that others didn't know one was bearing them.

"What time do you get off?"

"One o'clock. I'm off tomorrow, so I'm going out to get the baby."

"I'll be back and take you. Then we can talk."

He turned to Mrs. Dupree. "And a good day to you, too, madam." Bailey did little things with such a flourish. He might have been the Count of Monte Cristo, or Cyrano saying farewell to fair Roxanne.

After he had gone, Mrs. Dupree grinned her lips into a pucker. "He's as cute as a little bug."

I busied myself amid the pots. If she thought likening my big brother to an insect would please me, she had another think coming.

THE baby crawled around the floor of my room as I told Bailey of my great love affair. Of the pain of discovery of pain. He nodded understanding and said nothing.

I thought that while I had his attention I might as well throw in my other sadness. I told him that because my old schoolmates laughed at me, I felt more isolated than I had in Stamps, Arkansas.

He said, "He sounds like a nice guy" and "I think it's time for you to leave San Francisco. You could try Los Angeles or San Diego."

"But I don't know where I'd live. Or get a job." Although I was miserable in San Francisco, the idea of any other place frightened me. I thought of Los Angeles and it was a gray vast sea without ship or lighthouse.

"I can't just tear Guy away. He's used to the woman who looks after him."

"But she's not his mother."

"I've got a good job here."

"But surely you don't mean to make cooking Creole food your life's work."

I hadn't thought about it. "I have a nice room here. Don't you think it's nice?"

He looked at me squarely, forcing me to face my fears. "Now, My, if you're happy being miserable, enjoy it, but don't ask me to feel sorry for you. Just get all down in it and wallow around. Take your time to savor all its subtleties, but don't come to me expecting sympathy."

He knew me too well. It was true. I was loving the role of jilted lover. Deserted, yet carrying on. I saw myself as the heroine, solitary, standing under a streetlight's soft yellow glow. Waiting. Waiting. As the fog comes in, a gentle rain falls but doesn't drench her. It is just enough to make her shiver in her white raincoat (collar turned up). Oh, he knew me too well.

"If you want to stay around here looking like death eating a soda cracker, that's your business. There are some rights no one has the right to take from you. That's one. Now, what do you want to do?"

That evening I decided to go to Los Angeles. At first I thought I'd work another month, saving every possible penny. But Bailey said, "When you make up your mind to make a change you have to follow through on the wave of decision." He promised me two hundred dollars when his ship paid off and suggested that I tell my boss that I'd be leaving in a week.

I had never had two hundred dollars of my own. It sounded like enough to live on for a year.

The prospect of a trip to Los Angeles returned my youth to me.

My mother heard my plans without surprise. "You're a woman. You can make up your own mind." She hadn't the slightest idea that not only was I not a woman, but what passed for my mind was animal instinct. Like a tree or a river, I merely responded to the winds and the tides.

She might have seen that, but her own mind was misted with the knowledge of a failing marriage, and the slipping away of the huge sums of money which she had enjoyed and thought her due. Her fingers still glittered with diamonds and she was a weekly customer at the most expensive shoe store in town, but her pretty face had lost its carefree adornment and her smile no longer made me think of day breaking.

"Be the best of anything you get into. If you want to be a whore, it's your life. Be a damn good one. Don't chippy at anything. Anything worth having is worth working for."

It was her version of Polonius' speech to Laertes. With that wisdom in my pouch, I was to go out and buy my future.

CHAPTER 8

THE Los Angeles Union Railway Terminal was a marvel of
Moorish, Spanish glamour. The main waiting room was vast
and the ceiling domed its way up to the clouds. Long curved
benches sat in dark wooden splendor, and outside its arched
doors, palm trees waved in lovely walks. Inlaid blue and
yellow tiles were to be found on every wall, arranged in gay
and exotic design.

It was easy to distinguish San Franciscans detraining amid
the crowd. San Franciscan women always, but always, wore
gloves. Short white snappy ones in the day, and long black or
white kid leather ones at night. The Southern Californians
and other tourists were much more casual. Men sported flow-
ered shirts, and women ambled around or lounged on the
imposing seats in cotton dresses which could have passed for
brunch coats in San Francisco.

Being from The City, I had dressed for the trip. A black
crepe number which pulled and pleated, tucked and shirred,
in a wrap all its own. It was expensive by my standards and

dressy enough for a wedding reception. My short white gloves had lost their early-morning crispness during the ten-hour coach trip, and Guy, whose immensity matched his energy, had mashed and creased and bungled the dress into a very new symmetry. Less than a year old, he had opinions. He definitely wanted to get down and go to that smiling stranger across the aisle, and immediately wanted to be in my lap pulling on the rhinestone brooch which captured and brought light to the collar of my dress.

In spite of the wrinkled dress and in spite of the cosmetic case full to reeking with dirty diapers, I left the train with my son a picture of controlled dignity. I had over two hundred dollars rolled in scratchy ten-dollar bills in my brassiere, another seventy in my purse, and two bags of seriously selected clothes. Los Angeles was going to know I was there.

MY aunt answered my telephone call.

"Ritie, where are you?"

"We're at the station."

"What we?"

Like all the family she had heard about my pregnancy, but she hadn't seen the result.

"My son and I."

A tiny hesitation, then: "Get a taxi and come out here. I'll pay the cab fare." Her voice didn't ooze happiness at hearing from me, but then, the Baxters were not known to show any emotions. Except violent ones.

Wilshire Boulevard was wide and glossy. Large buildings sat back on tiny little lawns in a privacy that projected money and quiet voices and white folks.

The house on Federal Avenue had a no-nonsense air

about it. It was a model of middle-class decorum. A single-story, solidly made building with three bedrooms, good meant-to-last furniture, and samplers on the wall which exhorted someone to "Bless This Home" and warned that "Pride Goeth Before a Fall."

The clan had met, obviously called by my aunt, to check out my new addition to the family and give me the benefit of their conglomerate wisdom. My Uncle Tommy sat, wide-spraddled as usual, and grumbled. "Hey, Ritie. Got a baby, I see."

Guy was in my arms and talking, pointing, laughing, so the meaning in his statement was not in the words. He was simply greeting me and saying that although I had a child without benefit of marriage, he for one was not going to ignore either me or the baby.

My family spoke its own mysterious language. The wives and husbands of my blood relatives handed my son around as if they were thinking of adding him to their collection. They removed his bootees and pulled his toes.

"Got good feet."

"Uh huh. High arches."

One aunt ran her hand around his head and was satisfied. "His head is round."

"Got a round head, huh?"

"Sure does."

"That's good."

"Uh huh."

This feature was more than a symbol of beauty. It was an indication of the strength of the bloodline. Every Baxter had a round head.

"Look a lot like Bibbi, doesn't he?" "Bibbi" was the family

name for my mother. Guy was handed around the circle again.

"Sure does."

"Yes. I see Bibbi right here."

"Well . . . but he's mighty fair, isn't he?"

"Sure is."

They all spoke without emotion, except for my Aunt Leah. Her baby voice rose and fell like music played on a slender reed.

"Reetie, you're a woman now. A mother and all that. You'll have two to think of from now on. You'll have to get a job—"

"I've been working as a cook." She shouldn't think I had come to be taken care of.

"—and learn to save your money."

Tommy's wife, Sarah, wrapped my son carefully in his blanket and handed him to me. Aunt Leah stood, a signal that the inspection was over. "What time is your train? Charlie can drive you to the station."

My brain reeled. Had I given the impression that I was going on? Did they say something I missed? "In a few hours. I should be getting back."

We were all shaking hands. Their relief was palpable. I was, after all, a Baxter and playing the game. Being independent. Expecting nothing and if asked, not giving a cripple crab a crutch.

Tom asked, "Need some money, Reet?"

"No thanks. I've got money." All I needed was to get away from that airless house.

My uncles and aunts were childless, except for my late Uncle Tuttie, and they were not equipped to understand that an eighteen-year-old mother is also an eighteen-year-old girl. They were a close-knit group of fighters who had no patience with weakness and only contempt for losers.

I was hurt because they didn't take me and my child to their bosom, and because I was a product of Hollywood upbringing and my own romanticism. On the silver screen they would have vied for me. The winner would have set me up in a cute little cottage with frangipani and roses growing in the front yard. I would always wear pretty aprons and my son would play in the Little League. My husband would come home (he looked like Curly) and smoke his pipe in the den as I made cookies for the Boy Scouts meeting.

I was hurt because none of this would come true. But only in part. I was also proud of them. I congratulated myself on having absolutely the meanest, coldest, craziest family in the world.

Uncle Charlie, Aunt Leah's husband, never talked much, and on the way back to that station he broke the silence only a few times.

"You sure got yourself a cute baby."

"Thank you."

"Going on to San Diego, huh?"

I guessed so.

"Well, your father's down there. You won't be by yourself."

My father, who spent his time drinking tequila in Mexico and putting on high-toned airs in San Diego, would give me a colder reception than the one I'd just received.

I would be by myself. I thought how nice it would be.

I decided that one day I would be included in the family legend. Someday, as they sat around in the closed circle recounting the fights and feuds, the prides and prejudices of the Baxters, my name would be among the most illustrious. I would become a hermit. I would seal myself off from the world, just my son and I.

I had written a juicy melodrama in which I was to be the star. Pathetic, poignant, isolated. I planned to drift out of the wings, a little girl martyr. It just so happened that life took my script away and upstaged me.

CHAPTER 9

"ARE you in the life?"

The big black woman could have been speaking Russian. She sat with her back to the window and the sunlight slid over her shoulders, making a pool in her lap.

"I beg pardon?"

"The life. You turn tricks?"

The maid at the hotel had given me the woman's address and said she took care of children. "Just ask for Mother Cleo."

She hadn't asked me to sit, so I just stood in the center of the cluttered room, the baby resting on my shoulder.

"No. I do not." How could she ask me such a question?

"Well, you surely look like a trickster. Your face and everything."

"Well, I assure you, I'm not a whore. I have worked as a chef." How the lowly have become mighty. Ole Creole Kitchen would hitch up its shoulders to know that it once had had a chef—not just a garden-variety cook.

"Well." She looked at me as if she'd soon be able to tell if I was lying.

"How come you got so much powder and lipstick?" That morning I had bought a complete cosmetic kit and spent over an hour pasting my face into a mask with Max Factor's Pancake No. 31. I didn't really feel I had to explain to Mother Cleo, but on the other hand I couldn't very well be rude. I did need a baby-sitter.

"Maybe I put on too much."

"Where do you work?"

It was an interrogation. She had her nerve. Did she think that being called Mother Cleo gave her maternal privileges?

"The Hi Hat Club needs a waitress. I'm going to apply." The make-up was supposed to make me look older. Maybe it only succeeded in making me look cheap.

"That's a good job. Tips can make it a real good job. Let me see the baby."

She got up with more ease than I had expected. When she stretched out her hands a cloud of talcum powder was released. She took the baby and adjusted him down in the crook of her arm. "He's pretty. Still sleeping, huh?"

Mother Cleo metamorphosed in front of me. She was no longer the ugly fat ogre who threatened from her deep chair. Looking down on the infant, she had become the prototype of mother. Her face softened and her voice blurred. She ran stubbly fat fingers around his cap and slid it off.

"I don't usually take them this young. Too much trouble. But he's cute as can be, ain't he?"

"Well, you know—"

"Don't do for you to say so, but still it's true. And you're almost too young to have a baby. I guess your folks put you out, huh?"

She had noticed I wore no wedding ring. I decided to let

her think I was homeless. Then I thought, "Let her think nothing. I was homeless."

"Well, I'm going to give you a hand. I'll keep him and I'm going to charge you less than the white ones." I was shocked that she kept white babies. "Lots of white women trust their babies with me rather than they own mothers. There lot of them from the South and they like the idea that they still got a mammy for they children. Can't you just see them? Snotty-nosed little things growing up talking about 'I had a colored mammy.' Huh?" She uglied her face with wrinkles. "But I naturally like children and I make they mommas pay. They pay me good. Don't care how much I like they young 'uns, they don't pay they have to go."

I agreed to her terms and paid her for the first week. Before I left, the baby struggled awake in her arms. She began a rocking motion which didn't lull him. His large black eyes took in the strange face and he began to look around for me. A small cry found its way to the surface before I came into his vision. Once he had assured himself that indeed I was there, he hollered in earnest, angry that I had allowed him to be held by this unknown person, and maybe even a little afraid that I'd given him away. I moved to take him.

"Let him cry." Mother Cleo increased her rocking and bouncing. "He got to get used to it."

"Just let me hold him a second." I couldn't bear his loneliness. I took his softness and kissed him and patted his back and he quieted immediately, as a downpour of rain cuts off.

"You too soft. They all do that till they get used to me." She stood near me and held out her arms. "Give him to me and you go on and get your job. I'll feed him. You bring diapers?"

I nodded to the bag I had dropped beside the door.

"Hush baby, hush baby, hush baby, hush." She had started to croon. I handed the baby to her and right away he began to cry.

"Go on. He'll be all right."

He yelled louder, splitting the air with screams. She contrived a wordless song. His screams were lightning, piercing the dark cloud of her music. I closed the door.

CHAPTER 10

THE night club sat on the corner, a one-story building whose purple stucco façade was sprinkled with glitter dust. Inside the dark square room, a bar dimly curved its way from the door to a small dance floor in the rear. Minuscule round tables and chairs jammed against one another, and red bulbs shone down, intensifying the gloom.

The Hi Hat Club had almost too much atmosphere.

Music blared and trembled, competing with the customers' voices for domination of the air. Neither won, except that for a few seconds during the lull between records, the jukebox sat quiet up against the wall, its green and red and yellow lights flickering like an evil robot from a Flash Gordon film.

The customers came mostly from the underworld, though there was a scattering of young sailors among them. They all jockeyed and shifted, lifting glasses and voices in the thick air, which smelled of Lysol and perfume and bodies, and cigarettes and stale beer. The women were mistresses of decorum. They sat primly at the bar, skirts tucked in, voices quick or silent altogether. On the street they had been as ageless as their profession, but near the posturing, flattering men, they became modest girls. Kittens purring under the strokes.

I watched them and understood. I saw them and envied. They had men of their own. Of course they bought them. They laid open their bodies and threw away their dignity upon a heap of come-filled rubbers. But they had men.

In the late evenings, boosters and thieves wove their paths among the night people, trading, bartering, making contacts and taking orders.

"Got two Roos Bros. suits. Thirty-eight. Black. Pinstripe and nigger-brown. Tag says one-ninety dollars . . . they both yours for an ace fifty."

"Gelman shoes. I. Magnin dresses. Your woman'll catch if she wear these threads. For you, four dresses for a deuce."

Depending on the evening's take and the sweet man's mood, the thieves were given money by the pimps which had been given them by the girls which they had saved by lying down first and getting up last.

The waitresses, in a block, were the least interesting of the club's inhabitants. They were for the most part dull married women, who moved among the colorful patrons like slugs among butterflies. The men showed no interest in them, leading me to believe that virtue is safest in a den of iniquity.

I was younger but no more interesting than my colleagues, so the pretty men lumped me with them and ignored us all.

I had no chance to show them how clever I was because wit is communicated by language and I hadn't yet learned theirs. I understood their lack of interest to imply that smart women were prostitutes and stupid ones were waitresses. There were no other categories.

I worked cleaning ashtrays, serving drinks and listening

for over a month. My tips were good because I was fast and had a good memory.

"Scotch and milk for you, sir?"

"That's right, little girl, you got a good memory." Though he never saw me, he'd leave a dollar tip.

My first week in San Diego, Mother Cleo had told me she had a room for rent. "I see you a good girl coming over here to see your baby ever day and all, so my husband and me, we ready to let you live here with us. Room'll be fifteen dollars a week. Got a new bedroom suite in it and if you put a rubber sheet on the bed, your baby can sleep with you." So I became a roomer in the home of Mr. Henry and Mrs. Cleo Jenkins.

My life began to move at a measured tempo. I found a modern dance studio where a long-haired white woman gave classes to a motley crew of Navy wives.

I went to work at six (five-thirty to set up tables, get change, arrange my tray with napkins and matches) and was off at two. I shared a ride with a waitress whose husband picked her up every night. I slept late, woke to fix my break-fast around noon and play with my baby.

He amused me. I could not and did not consider him a person. A real person. He was my baby, rather like a pretty living doll that belonged to me. I was myself too young and unformed a human being to think of him as a human being. I loved him. He was cute. He laughed a lot and gurgled and he was mine.

CHAPTER 11

———— ≋ ————

I HAD begun to look forward to two women coming in every night. They were both just under thirty, and separately they would not have attracted much attention. Johnnie Mae was thin, taller than average, dark-brown-skinned. Her long jaw sagged down, giving her a look of sadness even when she laughed. She wore fuchsia lipstick and most often showed pink smudges on her long white teeth.

Beatrice was plump to ripening. A short yellow woman whose role seemed to be straight man to Johnnie Mae's unfunny but loud humor.

The fact that the pimps and panderers didn't harass them, bespoke the tolerance in the black community for people who chose to lead lives different from the norm. Although they were obviously not sisters, they dressed identically and never spoke to anyone except each other and me.

"Good evening, ladies. Two Tom Collins, I presume." I was a democrat and treated every lady the same.

"Evening, Rita. That's right." They must have spent their free time practicing before mirrors. They sounded alike and even the looks on one face were reflected on the other.

"Got you running this evening, ain't they?" The question did not really need answering. My tray was always filled with fresh drinks, dirty ashtrays or empty glasses.

"When you going to come over to our house?" They smiled at each other, then gave me their sly glances.

"Well, I work all the time, you know."

"Yes, but you have a day off. You say you don't have any friends here."

"I'm thinking about it. That'll be two dollars, please."

Lesbians still interested me, but I no longer felt tenderly protective of them: when I was fifteen I had spent nearly a year concerning myself with society's gross mistreatment of hermaphrodites. I was anxious over the plight of lesbians during the time I was consumed with fear that I might be an incipient one. Their importance to me had diminished in direct relationship to my assurance that I was not.

"Johnnie Mae got something nice for you yesterday."

"Sure did."

"It's a birthday surprise."

"But you don't know my birthday."

"That's how come it's a surprise."

They laughed into each other's laugh and I was forced to join them. Customers at other tables needed my attention, but the two women stayed on the fringes of my mind as I laced myself around the room. They weren't frightening, and they were funny.

"We'll get a bottle of Dubonnet"—Beatrice pronounced it doo bonnet— "for you and I'll cook. You're off on Sunday. Come over and I'll fry a Sunday bird."

"And we can have a ham."

"Just the three of us? Chicken and ham?" That was a lot of food.

"Nigger ham. A watermelon." Their laughter, crackling, met in the air above the table.

"I take my baby out on Sundays."

They thought about that while I waited on the other customers.

"You can bring him over."

"I'll think about it."

At the bar a thick-waisted waitress who had never invited me to her house curled her upper lip.

"You'd better be careful." She sent a hostile glance to Johnnie Mae's table.

"Why?" I wanted to hear her say it.

"Those women. You know what they are?" Her voice had taken on a sinister depth.

"What?"

"Bull daggers." She smirked her satisfaction at saying the word.

"Oh, really?" I put no surprise in my voice.

"You know about bull daggers, don't you?" Her face showed how her tongue relished the words.

"They dag bulls?" For a second she wasn't sure if I was being smart.

"They love women."

"Oh, is that all? That's all right then. They don't scare me. They can't eat me up." I flounced away, leaving my tray on the bar, and went directly to the table.

"Listen. I'm not a . . . not . . . not a lesbian, and I don't want to be one. Is that all right?"

Their faces closed. Johnnie Mae asked, "Is what all right?"

Suddenly I was ashamed. "I mean, I'd like to come to your

house on Sunday. But ... I mean, I wanted you to know that ... I don't go that way."

They were silent, wind-up toys whose springs had broken. I wished I could catch the words and swallow them whole.

"I'd like your address." I held out my pencil. Johnnie Mae took it and handed it to Beatrice.

"What time on Sunday?" I had to put something into the emptiness. Beatrice was writing.

"Two o'clock. When we come from church," said Johnnie Mae, handing me the paper.

"Okee dokee. See you then." I wanted to be flippant, to be funny, to say something that would erase the sadness, but I could think of nothing. I got my tray and went back to work.

CHAPTER 12

ON the blocks where Saturday-night revelers rambled, Sunday afternoons were given over to the godly. They filled the streets with a mighty thronging, vestiges of a recent contact with God, the Father, lying brightly on a few faces. Most gossiped, shared confidences, checked others' Sunday go-to-meeting clothes, and then spun from the crowd to head homeward.

Growing up, becoming responsible, having to think ahead and assuming the postures of adulthood had certain compensations for me. One that I weekly appreciated was the freedom to sleep late on Sundays. (Somehow the bed was more sensual on that morning then weekdays.) I loved the soul-stirring songs and heartily approved of the minister's passions, but being penned shoulder to shoulder with a rocking crowd of strangers for three hours or more did nothing for my soul.

I maneuvered through the churchgoers, listening for and hearing:

"The Reverend sure spoke today."

"That's the truth, child. He did it today."

"Reverend was talking to my soul this morning."

"Bless your heart. Mine too."

"It's a wonderful thing to go into the house of the Lord."

"That's the truth."

The sounds waved like pretty ribbons and belonged to me.

I understood them all. I was a part of that crowd. The fact of my Southern upbringing, the fact of my born blackness meant that I was for the rest of my life a member of that righteous band, and would be whether or not I ever went to church again.

THE small white house sat squarely in a dirt yard. A few roses tried vainly to grow along a wire fence.

Johnnie Mae opened the door and from her taut smile I knew my blunt words of the other night might have been forgiven, but they were not forgotten.

Beatrice came from the rear of the house and stood beside Johnnie Mae. Both of them talked at once.

"You made it. We didn't think you were going to. We just got back from church. Just changed our clothes." They had changed into matching white T-shirts and pedal pushers.

In Southern towns, the people my grandmother called "wordly" socialized on Saturday night, while the "godly" entertained and were entertained in cool parlors on Sunday. The black people brought that custom north along with their soft speech and remembered recipes. Since my hostesses and I were Southern, I expected to sit at an overloaded table giving fulsome compliments while they plied me with "just one more helping."

"Come in. Take the weight off. Hope you're not starving.

I'm just starting to cook." They were as nervous as I. I moved into the tiny room and immediately felt too big for it.

"Thought you were going to bring the baby."

"He was asleep. I'll go back early and take him for a walk." That was going to be my excuse to get away.

"Well, what do you think of our house?" I hadn't had a chance to look around before. I noticed that the walls were bare and there were no books, but furniture they had plenty. A fat, overstuffed rust sofa pressed its matching chair into a corner. Two large chairs, more accidental than incidental, stood pompous against the other wall. Little clear glass lamps, topped with white frilly shades, sat on two end tables. Things took up all the air.

"Come on, see the rest before you sit down." Johnnie Mae's pride carried us into a bedroom while Beatrice went back to the kitchen.

"Have you ever slept in a round bed before?" I hadn't and I hadn't seen one either. It didn't seem appealing, although it was covered with a blue satin spread which matched its curves.

"When Beatrice has her flowers she sleeps in here." I followed her into a monastic cell. A small cot and an old dresser were the room's only furnishings. No lamps, no doilies.

"Her flowers?" I wasn't really so curious as I was uncomfortable.

Johnnie Mae said, "Her monthlies. I don't get them any more. I had an operation. If she wasn't so scared of hospitals, she'd have one too."

"An operation?" I was young, but I was also stupid.

"Had my ovaries and all that mess taken out; Bee ought to get it done too. After all, I'm not about to give her any babies, am I? She hunched me and winked. I must have returned the wink. I don't know. But I was thinking of the stupidity which got me in the predicament. The big generous unprejudiced spirit which had got me hooked up with two lesbians of heavy humor.

"It's nice. Your house is really very nice. I mean, it reflects your taste and your personalities. I always say, if you want to know a woman, I mean a person, go to their house. It will tell you . . ." I knew that words, despite the old saying, never fail. And my reading had given me words to spare. I could, and often did to myself or my baby, recite whole passages of Shakespeare, Paul Lawrence Dunbar poems, Kipling's "If," Countee Cullen, Langston Hughes, Longfellow's *Hiawatha*, Arna Bontemps. Surely I had enough words to cover a moment's discomfort. I had enough for hours if need be.

Back on the prickly sofa, Johnnie Mae offered me Dubonnet. I held the glass of thick sweet wine as protection. Thinking she would hesitate to pounce on me if there was a chance I would spill the wine on her furniture, I kept it in front of me like a shield.

"Beatrice, come out here. You're not chained to the stove." She looked at me and raised thick eyebrows. Johnnie Mae had the infuriating habit of making anyone she spoke to into a fellow conspirator. I raised my eyebrows back at her as if I understood her meaning. Beatrice came into the room, a sprinkling of perspiration dotting her face.

"Now, baby, you don't want no black chicken do you?" Beatrice was teasing. Flirting.

"If that chicken gets any darker than you, I'll have to whip your rusty dusty." They were a comedy team. If I had heard that exchange at the club I would have joined their laughter, but perched guarded in the cluttered room, I couldn't find anything funny. I laughed.

"Come here, you sweet thing." Beatrice obeyed and stood like a little chubby girl in front of Johnnie Mae.

"Bend down." Johnnie Mae raised her face and the two women's lips met. I watched and saw their tongues snaking in and out. Except in movies I had never even seen men and women kiss passionately. They pulled apart and looked at me in a practiced gesture. For a second I was too embarrassed to have been caught watching, and in the next second I knew they had wanted me to see. Even after I told them I had no interest in lesbianism, they thought the sight of women kissing would excite me.

I hated their stupidity, but more than that I hated being underestimated. If they only knew, they could strip buck naked and do the Sassy Sue wiggle and I would continue to sit, with my legs crossed, sipping the Dubonnet.

Beatrice's laughter floated over her shoulder as she headed back to the kitchen. Johnnie Mae looked at me and by leering tried to include me in her appreciation.

"Beatrice would make a rabbit hug a hound." She grunted like a pig.

Because laughter seemed to be the safest sport in the house, I laughed and said, "Where do you work? I mean both of you?"

"Right here. Flat on our backs." Nothing embarrassed the women. "We both take two all-night tricks apiece once a week. Comes to two hundred dollars. We more than get by." She indicated the sofa and chairs. "As you can see."

Lesbian prostitutes! Did they trick with women? I ached to know. How did they pick them up? I had never heard of women hustling other women, but surely they didn't go to bed with men. I fished for a way to put my question.

Johnnie Mae looked around the room, her eyes counting

and loving the many pieces of furniture. Her head finished its semicircle and I was back in her vision.

"We're going to have to move, you know?" The question was foolish. Not only did I not know, I didn't care. And if I'd had the chance to think about it, I'd have thought it was a good thing, too.

"The landlord doesn't like us. He's a church deacon, he says. But the real reason is that his son is a faggot. Goes around wearing women's clothes, so the old bastard can't stand gay people." She was happy to grin, thinking of the man's unhappiness. "I told the old bastard so, too." She shrugged her shoulders against the fates. "We'll find another place. I hate to move, though. I mean, we painted this place ourselves." The walls were pea-yellow in the living room. "We called this our honeymoon cottage. Beatrice planted the roses."

I felt there was something I was supposed to say. Something like "You have my deepest sympathy." For some reason, at that moment I thought about Curly and did in fact feel sorry for the two women.

"Niggers make me sick. And nigger men make me sicker than that." She might have been thinking of her landlord, but it seemed she was reading my mind and had the audacity to mean Curly. She would have lost my sympathy, anyway. I hated the word "nigger" and never believed it to be a term of endearment, no matter who used it.

"Now you tell me. We been wondering about you. How come you working as a waitress? You speak such good English, you must have a diploma."

"Yes, I do." Shock pushed my voice out.

"You mean you graduated from high school?"

"Yes."

"And work as a waitress?"

"Well, I can't type or take shorthand or—"

"You remind me of Beatrice." She shouted, "Beatrice. Come here." I feared I was going to have to sit through the kissing again.

Beatrice stood at the door leading to the living room. "What's on your mind?"

Johnnie Mae didn't have time for fun. "Bee, Rita's just like you. She finished high school."

Beatrice, knowing that wasn't such a grand feat said, "Really. Got your diploma, huh?"

Johnnie Mae answered for me. "Sure she got it. And works as a waitress." I started to explain, but she stopped me. "Beatrice was a WAC. A corporal." It was hard to believe that all that soft-looking flesh had been contained in an army uniform. "And when she got out she went to work. That's where we met. At some rich old woman's house. Bee was the cook and I was the housekeeper. I took one look at Bee and I have been keeping her ever since."

Break for peals of laughter.

CHAPTER 13

———————— ⟣ ————————

"LET'S have a little grifa before dinner." Johnnie Mae gave an order, not an invitation. She turned to me.

"You like grifa?"

"Yes. I smoke." The truth was I had smoked cigarettes for over a year, but never marijuana. But since I had the unmitigated gall to sit up cross-legged in a lesbian apartment sipping wine, I felt I had the stamina to smoke a little grifa. Anyway, I was prepared to refuse anything else they offered me, so I didn't feel I could very well refuse the pot.

Beatrice laid down a Prince Albert can on the table with cigarette papers.

"Do you want to roll it?" Johnnie Mae was being gracious.

"No thanks. I don't roll very well." I hadn't seen loose tobacco and cigarette papers since I'd left the South, five years earlier. My brother and I used to roll lumpy cigarettes for my uncle on a small hand-cranking machine when he'd run out of ready rolls.

She took the papers and deftly began to sift marijuana. I

tried not to appear too curious as the grains of tobacco fell into the cupped paper.

"I'd like to use your bathroom."

"Sure. You know where it is."

I talked to the bathroom mirror. "You have nothing to be nervous about. You'll get out of this. Don't you always get out of everything? Marijuana is not habit-forming. Thousands of people have smoked it. The Indians and Mexicans and it didn't send them mad. Just wash your hands"—which were damp—"and go back to the living room. Keep your cool. Cool."

I inhaled the smoke as casually as if the small brown cigarette I held were the conventional commercial kind.

"No. No. Don't waste the grifa. Hand it here." She dragged the cigarette and made the sound of folks slurping tea from a saucer.

"But I like it my way." Stubborn to the end.

"Well, try it like this." Again the rattling sound.

"All right. I will." I opened my throat and kept my tongue flat so that the smoke found no obstacle in its passage from my lips to my throat. It tore the lining off my tonsils, made my nasal passages burn like red pepper and choked me. While I coughed, gagging, those silly bitches laughed. They would be sitting there with those vapid wrinkles on their faces while I choked to death. Wouldn't they do anything for me? No. Beatrice rescued the joint and sucked in the smoke, puffing out her already fat cheeks to bursting, while her lady love was busily engaged in rolling another stick of tearing fire.

Before the cough stopped shaking me, I had decided I would get even with them. They were lesbians, which was sinful enough, but they were also inconsiderate, stupid bitches. I reached again for the marijuana.

The food was the best I'd ever tasted. Every morsel was an experience of sheet delight. I lost myself in a haze of sensual pleasure, enjoying not only the tastes but the feel of the food in my mouth, the smells, and the sound of my jaws chewing.

"She's got a buzz. That's her third helping."

I looked up to see the two women looking at me and laughing. Their faces seemed to be mostly teeth. White teeth staggering inside dark lips. They were embarrassingly ugly, and yet there was something funny about it. They had no idea that they were so strange-looking. I laughed at their ignorance, and they, probably thinking themselves to be laughing at mine, joined me. When I remembered how they were ready to let me choke to death and how I vowed to get them, the tears rolled down my cheeks. That was really funny. They didn't know what I was thinking and I didn't know what form my revenge would take.

"Let's have some sounds." Beatrice got up from the table. We were by magic back in the murky living room. Johnnie Mae stood putting records on the player. She turned to me as the first record began to play. "You said you're studying how to dance. Do us a dance." Lil Green's voice whined out the sadful lyrics:

> "In the dark, in the dark, I get such a thrill
> when you press your fingertips upon my lils."

I COULDN'T explain that I didn't do dancing alone to music like that. At the studio I did stretches, extensions, pliés and relevés to Prokofiev, Tchaikovsky and Stravinsky.

It was considered normal in gatherings to ask a child or even an adult to entertain. The talented person was expected to share his gift. The singer was asked to "Sing us a little song!" and the person with a gift of memorizing was asked to "Render us a poem!" In my mother's house I had often been called to show what I was studying at dance school. The overstuffed chairs were pulled back and I would dance in the cleared living-room space. I hummed inaudibly and moved precisely from ballet position one straight into a wobbling arabesque. Mother's company would set their highballs down to applaud.

I decided to dance for my hostesses. The music dipped and swayed, pulling and pushing. I let my body rest on the sound and turned and bowed in the tiny room. The shapes and forms melted until I felt I was in a charcoal sketch, or a sepia watercolor.

When the record finished I stopped. The two women sat on the sofa. Made solemn.

"That was good. Wasn't it, baby?"

"Sure was."

"Dance with Beatrice. I don't mind. Go on. Beatrice, dance with Rita."

Again, order was in her voice. The last thing in the world I wanted to do was dance with another woman. Johnnie Mae got up and started the Lil Green song again and Beatrice moved up close to me. She put her arm around my waist and took my left hand as if we were going to waltz. It was crushing. Not only was she fat and soft and a head shorter than I, her big breasts rubbed against my stomach. She stuck her thigh between my knees and we wobbled around the room.

This was the ultimate insult. I would vent my spleen on those thick-headed lecherous old hags. They couldn't do me this way and get away with it.

"That's right, Beatrice, do the dip." The woman did a fancy step and bent back, pulling me with her. I nearly toppled over. Mercifully, the record finished after what seemed one thousand hours and I was allowed to return to the sofa.

"You all look good together. Beatrice can sure dance, can't she? Come here, baby, and give me a kiss."

I got up and made room for Beatrice.

"No. You can stay." She encircled Beatrice, whose face was heavy with submission.

"Have to go to the toilet again." Let the mental machine do its work. In the bathroom an idea bloomed. They were whores. Why not encourage them in their chosen profession? From what I understood, whores can never get enough money, and since they had so little, I dressed my newborn creation carefully and took it back to the living room. I asked if we could turn down the music because I wanted to talk.

"Rita wants to talk." They broke out of their embrace. Nasty things.

"I just thought I might be able to help you keep this place. You like it so much and you've made it so cute, it'd be a shame if you lost it."

They nearly became maudlin in their agreement.

"Well, I could rent it, and you could continue to stay."

"You mean you pay the rent and we pay you back."

"No. I'll rent the place in my name, I'll have the lights and gas put in my name. And pay everything. And three nights a week or four nights a week, you all stay here and turn tricks."

Beatrice's silly little voice complained: "You mean to turn our home into a whorehouse?"

Well, whores lived in it and it was a house. "Do you realize if the trade builds up, you can buy a place of your own and fix it just like this?" And they probably would.

"Where would we get the tricks?" Ever-practical Johnnie Mae.

"We'd get white taxi drivers and give them a percentage." My brain was clicking along like a Santa Fe train. A-hooting and a-howling. "They could be told the hours, like between ten and two. Then if every trick is twenty dollars, they get five and we split the fifteen. Seven-fifty for you. Seven-fifty for me."

"We don't want to be whores. I mean, full time." Old big little Beatrice already scared. What did she do in the WACS? Seduce young girls?

"Tricking four days a week isn't full time," I said. "And anyway, if you're successful, you can quit it in six months. Go and buy you a little place. Fact is, you could even get a bigger house." And get even more junk in it. "If all three of us save, do you realize we could open a restaurant in a year? Beatrice as the chef. You and I as managers."

I was getting to them. "I had a little operation up the coast. A three-girl deal, but I had to close down." Admiration and a little fear showed in their faces. They hadn't bargained for what they were getting.

Johnnie Mae, not wanting to believe what she already believed, asked, "Why were you working as a waitress?"

Should I tell them in order to eat and pay for my son's keep, so they'd throw me down on that uncomfortable sofa and rape me? "I needed a front. Cops after me."

"Cops!" Both of them screamed. Like many weak people they wanted to milk the cow, at the same time denying the smell of bullshit. I saw immediately that I had gone too far.

"Not after me myself. One of my girls, but I wanted to lay a cover for myself."

Beatrice said, "You're awfully young to be in the rackets."

"I've been around, baby." I rolled my eyes to indicate distant and mysterious places. "Well, how does it sound? Say we say Wednesday, Thursday, Friday and Saturday. Then you're free for church on Sunday and—"

"We'd better talk about it."

"I'm off tomorrow and I can get all the business taken care of. No time like the present."

"We only have the two bedrooms. Where will *you* work?"

I almost shouted at the tall woman. Me, turn tricks? What did she think I was? "I'm going to stay on at the restaurant. Shouldn't call attention to myself, you understand. But you won't be alone. I'll have somebody here to watch out for you. Just leave it to me."

I became pompously professional, which was never hard for me, being my father's daughter. "If you'll let me have a tablet and a pen, I'll take the landlord's address."

"Beatrice. Get some paper."

I moved over to the table, shifting the dinner dishes and crumbs out of my way as Johnnie Mae dictated.

"What's this address again?"

She gave it to me and I wrote it over and over on slips of paper.

"What you doing now?" Johnnie Mae wasn't bright, but she'd always be too clever to just go for the okey-doke. I put it in my mind that I'd better keep that in mind.

"When I leave here, I'm going to start drumming up business," I said. "In a few weeks we'll be thousandaires."

"What?"

"That's just a step from millionaires. Let's have a drink on it." Beatrice poured. The first mouthful nearly sent me reeling. It made contact with the grifa in my brain. For a lightning second I was sober with a clear recollection of what I had done, then blissfully I was high again. An authority in charge of affairs.

I said good-bye, alluded again to the wonderful food and the wonderful future we had in store, and walked out of the house.

I was certain that my heartlessness regarding the women stemmed from a natural need for revenge. After all my soggy sentimentality for the misunderstood, no one could have convinced me that I was merely acting out society's hate for the "other ones."

However, an irony struck me before I reached the little one-foot wire fence that guarded the pavement from the yard. In a successful attempt to thwart a seduction I had ended up with two whores and a whorehouse. And I was just eighteen.

CHAPTER 14

—————— ❧ ——————

"GOOD evening, driver."

"Yeah."

"Are there enough houses of ill repute to service the naval personnel?"

"Whaat?"

"I know you're generally paid four dollars on a twenty-dollar customer (I guessed, I didn't know), but if, after Thursday night ten-o'clock, you bring clients to this address, you'll be remunerated to the tune of five dollars per head."

You had to be very careful in speaking to whites, and especially white men. My mother said that when a white man sees your teeth he thinks he sees your underclothes.

I had managed in a few tense years to become a snob on all levels, racial, cultural and intellectual. I was a madam and thought myself morally superior to the whores. I was a waitress and believed myself cleverer than the customers I served. I was a lonely unmarried mother and held myself to be freer than the married women I met.

* * *

HANK was the club's erratic bouncer. Erratic because some-times he didn't show up, and other times, when his habits hit him, he bounced people onto the sidewalk who had done no more than offend his sensibilities. He spent a few nights monthly in the drunk tank, and was always taken back on his release.

The other waitresses hinted that Hank did a few private jobs for the boss. Secretly I believed the man was afraid of Hank, rightly, for there was no way to anticipate him. He might see in a stranger qualities of great worth, or he might develop an active hate for a person's color.

He had kind of adopted me on my arrival, and at the earliest opportunity I approached him. "Hank, I want to know if you'd look after some business for me?"

In another century that face would have so frightened a slave owner that he would have been compelled to lash the broad back and shackle the wide hands.

"Yeah, li'l sister. What's the matter?"

"You know the two les—bull daggers who come in here?"

"They ain't been messing with you, is they?"

"Oh no." The reverse. "They've asked me to back them in a business. Whorehouse, to be exact. Wednesday to Saturday. And you're the only person I can trust to watch out for my end. I figure to pay you one third of my take."

His mouth hung open. "You're going to be turning tricks?"

"Not me, I'm going to keep on working, but they will. Could you manage the place for me? Watch out for the police and keep track of the money?"

After much repeating myself, he agreed. I created an elaborate system of chits, which would be given to the women and the cabdrivers. At around two-thirty in the morning

Hank was to put on a porch light denoting a clear coast, and I would go in and pay off the workers.

I had a vague worry—that a sudden large bank account would put the vice squad on my trail. I wasn't afraid of the police, since I wasn't turning tricks myself, but I was terrified of how a police investigation would influence Mother Cleo. She'd toss me and my baby out of the house with much damning me to the depths of hell. There were other places to live of course, and with the money piling up in secret places I could afford anyone to tend my child, but the fact was that I cared for the Jenkinses and what they thought of me was important.

Their home and their ways reminded me of the grand-mother who raised me and whom I idolized. I wouldn't have them offended. When my illicit business reached its peak, I joined their church, and stood in the choir singing the old songs with great feeling.

One afternoon Mother Cleo remarked, "I know some-thing." And smiled a leer. Panic set in.

"What?"

"You doing something." She sang the accusation like schoolchildren promising to tell.

"What? I'm not doing anything." The ready lie at my tongue.

"You got yourself a fella."

Of all things, how could she come up with that? However wrong she was, I perceived she wasn't angry, and it would be safer to lie again.

I asked, "How did you know?" Pleased now that she had caught me.

" 'Cause you're coming in later than you used to. Me, I'm a light sleeper. Mr. Henry can sleep till the cows come home, but taking care of children makes me a light sleeper. I hear every footfall. You used to be in around two twenty-five, two-thirty. Now you get in sometimes its three-thirty. Am I right?"

"Yes."

"Well, is he a nice boy? Work where you work, don't he?"

"How do you know so much, Mother Cleo?"

" 'Cause anybody else couldn't stay up every night till you get off. If you want to, he can come 'round here to see you."

I started. "Not at night. But in the daytime, I don't mind." That was more like it. With so many unexpected things happening I would be very unhappy to see Mother Cleo's morals slip.

FOR two and a half months I operated at the points of a stylistic triangle, braggadocio (in front of the women) and modest servitude (at the club), and kept wondering what to do with all the cash.

I bought a car which was a model of Detroit genius. A pale-green Chrysler, '39 vintage, convertible. It sported wooden doors and highly polished wooden dashboards. Knobs and buttons were a yellow material like the handles of old-fashioned flatware. I fashioned a sling made out of belts and secured my son, who had begun to walk. We drove around the monotonous streets of San Diego in my beautiful chariot. I had paid cash for it from a dresser drawer of money.

Mother Cleo asked charily, "And where in the world . . . ?"

I had my answer molded. "My boyfriend gave it to me!"

"What'd he do? Steal it?"

"Oh no. He paid cash."

"How come he don't come around?"

"He's going to. I invited him." In fact, I had thought of

palming Hank off as the hard-working boyfriend but decided he'd never be able to carry it off.

"Listen here. He ain't a married man, is he?" She began to draw away from me as if I might be a carrier of a loathsome disease.

"No, ma'am. He's not even divorced. I mean, he's never been married."

She calmed down gradually, then her face hardened. "He ain't a white man, is he? I don't 'low white men."

I had to laugh. Of all the tricks who came and went in my establishment, I hadn't even seen one. "No, Mother Cleo, he's not even light-skinned."

Reluctantly she smiled. "One thing I don't hold with is women messing 'round with married mens. The other is messing 'round with white men. First one the Bible don't like, second one the law don't like."

She could have put her time to greater use concerning herself with my lack of morals rather than with my sexual involvements. Since coming to San Diego I let no attraction penetrate the invisible widow's weeds I had donned. My love was dead, my love was gone, married to some stupid shipfitter and living in the mosquito-ridden swamps of Louisiana. Long die, and stay dead, my love.

CHAPTER 15

DURING this time when my life hinged melodramatically on intrigue and deceit, I discovered the Russian writers. One title caught my eye. Not because I felt guilty raking in money from the doings of prostitutes but because of the title's perfect balance. Life, as far as I had deduced it, was a series of opposites: black/white, up/down, life/death, rich/poor, love/hate, happy/sad, and no mitigating areas in between. It followed Crime/Punishment.

The heavy opulence of Dostoevsky's world was where I had lived forever. The gloomy, lightless interiors, the complex ratiocinations of the characters, and their burdensome humors, were as familiar to me as loneliness.

I walked the sunny California streets shrouded in Russian mists. I fell in love with the Karamazov brothers and longed to drink from a samovar with the lecherous old father. Then Gorki became my favorite. He was the blackest, most dear, most despairing. The books couldn't last long enough for me. I wished the writers all alive, turning out manuscripts for my addiction. I took to the Chekov plays and Turgenev, but always returned in the late nights, after I had collected my boodle, to the Maxim Gorki and his murky, unjust world.

My dance teacher, who took no personal interest, wore the most outlandish clothes. Her long dark skirt, gathered, fell to just above her ankles. The blouses were of Mexican persuasion and were worn off her thin shoulders. Ropes of colorful beads and thong sandals completed her costume. She looked odd enough for admiration. I copied her clothes, and when not dressed in the white-blouse, black-skirt waitress uniform, I could be seen haunting the libraries, a tall thin black girl in too-long skirts and señorita blouses, which might have been sexy had I had the figure and/or attitude to complement them. Alas, I didn't.

Upon reflection, I marvel that no one saw through me enough to bundle me off to the nearest mental institution. The fact that it didn't happen depended less on my being a good actress than the fact that I was surrounded, as I had been all my life, by strangers. The world of waitress, dreamer, madam and mother might have continued indefinitely, except for another of life's unexpected surprises.

I didn't insist on any rules in my little whorehouse by the side of the road, except one: no all-night dates, no matter what the temptation. I wanted the money without name, the ease without strain. I never wanted any tricks to be in the house after I arrived, hence the signal with Hank.

One evening I sat in a taxi on the darkened street (I never took my automobile to the whorehouse) and waited for the light to go off on the porch. The driver, who also brought trade, and I walked into the house.

I stood in the center of the tiny living room, which smelled of Lysol and smoke and incense, hemmed in by the driver, the women and Hank, and by the furniture, which threatened to oust us all at any moment. Beatrice and Johnnie Mae erased any budding aspirations I had for owning things. Now that they had money, their acquisitive natures came into their own. The total filling up of the living room was so gradual that it was as if the existing furniture gave birth nightly to smaller and even larger images of itself.

Hank passed me the cigar box of money.

"Damn. Turn the damned radio off till we get business settled. You can't hear a shitting thing." I had taken to cursing to round out my image. The two women no longer took any interest in me, except possibly to hate my arrogance and envy my authority. I couldn't care less.

I had not finished recovering their chits and was about to turn to the cabdriver when a drunk, half-dressed white sailor stumbled through the bedroom door. He had nothing on below the blue middy. There was a moment's hush when the women and Hank looked at me. I was hypnotized at the man's nudity and couldn't take my eye's from his white, soft, dangling penis.

Beatrice ran to him. "Honey. I told you to stay—"

"What's going on? Who are all these folks?" His accent was lower Mississippi, and he looked as naked and white and ugly and drunk and nasty as anything I could think of.

Beatrice herded him back to the room.

In those seconds I became a child again. Unreasoning rage consumed me. The low-down sneaky bitches—I had told them to have the place cleared before I got there. They had probably had tricks there every night and I hadn't even questioned them. I could have gone to jail or worse. After all I'd done for them, their whorish hearts were so ungrateful that I had been subjugated to looking at the sickening aspect of a white man's penis.

I turned to Hank, and lumbering toward me, he said, "Rita, swear to God, I thought they was all gone."

Johnnie Mae allowed a little of her jealousy to show. "I don't see nothing wrong myself. You come over here every night collecting money, acting like you somebody's pimp. But you too good to turn a trick. And you keep this big rough sonofabitch watching us all the time. Well, you can kiss my black ass."

Her rudeness didn't surprise me. I would not have moved an eyebrow at anything any more. The driver stood mesmerized by the event.

I gave the cigar box to Hank. "Hank. Do you want a whorehouse, complete with whores? You've just been given one." I turned to the women, gathering all my injured dignity. "And, ladies, you decided in the beginning that you were going to screw me one way or the other. Look at us now. Who did the screwing?"

Beatrice's voice keened, sharpened and moved through the room like a swinging razor. "If it hadn't been for you, we'd be living like we always did."

"Yes, in the street, or back is some white woman's kitchen."

Johnnie Mae swelled up as if she had taken in more air than it was possible to release. "Be goddam careful how you talk to her, you big-nose bitch."

It was time to go. These lying heathens were not above attacking me. And after all I'd done for them.

"Hank, if you want this place, it's all yours." And one parting shot to the traitors: "At least I'm leaving you better off than I found you. You've got enough secondhand furniture to start your own Goodwill store." And to the cabdriver: "Will you please take me home."

I stood straighter, separating myself from the stench of my present environment, and started out. Johnnie Mae's rage propelled her after me. I reached the door just as she stretched her hand for me. I put on a little speed, not wanting to appear to be running, and escaped down the steps as she and the cab-driver collided in the doorway. He extricated himself in a hurry, more than a little terrified of getting caught between two restless tribes. Johnnie Mae, thwarted, for I had gained the sidewalk, screamed out into the quiet darkness, "You bitch! You think the police don't want to know how you bought that car. You better not drive it again. I'll have the vice squad on your ass."

I don't know how I continued walking to the cab. Her threat and the sound of her screech had stabbed me to the quick as surely as it had pierced the night. The wretch would put the cops on my trail and I'd lose my car, go to jail and be put out of Mother Cleo's. I was sitting in the back of the taxi when a numbing thought sidled across my brain like a poisonous snake. I might be declared an unfit mother and my son would be made a ward of the court. There were cases like that. In the cool early-morning air I began to sweat. The tiny glands in my armpits opened and closed to the pricking of a thousand straight pins.

"Please take me home, and I'm sorry for that terrible outburst." Fear still rode the front seat with the driver and he lost no time depositing me at my destination. I paid him, tipped him grandly and inundated him with praise for his reliability and courtesy, and lack of familiarity. I don't think he heard a word, and before I reached the front door, his tail lights had turned winking around the corner.

During the exotic buying sprees I hadn't thought to get luggage to hold my new acquisitions. I heaped piles of my clothes and my son's into the suitcases Bailey had given me in San Francisco. I had made up my mind that come daybreak, my son and I were going to make a run for it. If the police caught me, they'd catch me at the railway station or on the train, not a sitting duck waiting passively to be arrested. When I had finished cramming as many things as possible into the bags, I sat down to read until daybreak.

Since childhood I had often read until the gray light entered my room, but on that tense night it seemed sleep had allied itself with my enemies, and along with them was determined to overpower me, do me down. I tried sitting in a chair and sitting cross-legged on the bed. A knock awoke me. It was Mother Cleo.

"Rita, you left your light on again. You going to start helping me with the electricity. You don't know how much it cost . . ." She was moving away from the door, and her words reached down the hall.

I came to full attention and checked my luggage, my money and my story again.

"Mother Cleo, my mother is sick in San Francisco. She telephoned me at the club last night, so I have to go home." I had followed her into the kitchen. She put down her cup and looked at me with such sympathy I almost wished I wasn't lying.

"Oh, you poor thing. She ain't bad off, is she?"

"Oh no, nothing serious." I wanted to calm her fears.

"Well then, you won't be long. You'll leave the baby?"

"Oh no. She wants to see him. And I'll tell you the truth"—as if I could—"I'm not coming back soon."

"Aw, Don't tell me that. I've come to look on you as family."

"Mother Cleo, I appreciate everything you've done for us.

And I want you to have this." I laid fifty dollars on the table. "My boyfriend sent it to you as a present."

She beamed and I saw the tears start to form.

"Now, don't cry. We'll come back sometime. I wish you'd bathe the baby while I'm taking a bath, and then we'll hit the highway."

Her last words to me as she and Mr. Henry helped me to the car were attributes to my acting and successful deceit.

"You're just what I wanted for a daughter. You smart and mannerable and truthful. That's what I like most. You living a Christian life. Keep up the good work. God bless you and the child. And your mother."

I tore down the morning streets as if the hounds of hell were coming to collect my soul. The baby responded to the two-wheel curve-taking by giving out air-splitting screams. My "Hush, baby" and "It's all right, baby" could have been unheard whispers. He felt my panic and seemed to want the world to know that he was just as afraid as his mother.

At the train station I wiped the steering wheel and unstrapped the baby. I left the car parked in a No Parking zone, and as far as I know, it is there to this day.

I was racing away with my son on my hip and sheer fright in my heart. My general destination was the little village in Arkansas where I had grown up. But the particular goal of the journey was the protective embrace of Mrs. Annie Henderson, the grandmother who had raised me. Momma, as we called her, was a deliberately slow-speaking, right-thinking woman. And above all, she had what I lacked most at the moment. Courage.

CHAPTER 16

―――――――――― ✦ ――――――――――

THERE is a much-loved region in the American fantasy where pale white women float eternally under black magnolia trees, and white men with soft hands brush wisps of wisteria from the creamy shoulders of their lady loves. Harmonious black music drifts like perfume through this precious air, and nothing of a threatening nature intrudes.

The South I returned to, however, was flesh-real and swollen-belly poor. Stamps, Arkansas, a small hamlet, had subsisted for hundreds of years on the returns from cotton plantations, and until World War I, a creaking lumbermill. The town was halved by railroad tracks, the swift Red River and racial prejudice. Whites lived on the town's small rise (it couldn't be called a hill), while blacks lived in what had been known since slavery as "the Quarters."

After our parents' divorce in California, our father took us from Mother, put identification and destination tags on our wrists, and sent us alone, by train, to his mother in the South. I was three and my brother four when we first arrived in

Stamps. Grandmother Henderson accepted us, asked God for help, then set about raising us in His way. She had established a country store around the turn of the century, and we spent the Depression years minding the store, learning Bible verses and church songs, and receiving her undemonstrative love.

We lived a good life. We had some food, some laughter and Momma's quiet strength to lean against. During World War II the armed services drew the town's youth, black and white, and Northern war plants lured the remaining hale and hearty. Few, if any, blacks or poor whites returned to claim their heritage of terror and poverty. Old men and women and young children stayed behind to tend the gardens, the one paved block of stores and the long-accepted way of life.

In my memory, Stamps is a place of light, shadow, sounds and entrancing odors. The earth smell was pungent, spiced with the odor of cattle manure, the yellowish acid of the ponds and rivers, the deep pots of greens and beans cooking for hours with smoked or cured pork. Flowers added their heavy aroma. And above all, the atmosphere was pressed down with the smell of old fears, and hates, and guilt.

On this hot and moist landscape, passions clanged with the ferocity of armored knights colliding. Until I moved to California at thirteen I had known the town, and there had been no need to examine it. I took its being for granted and now, five years later, I was returning, expecting to find the shield of anonymity I had known as a child.

Along with other black children in small Southern villages, I had accepted the total polarization of the races as a psychological comfort. Whites existed, as no one denied, but they were not present in my everyday life. In fact, months often passed in my childhood when I only caught sight of the thin hungry po' white trash (sharecroppers), who lived sadder and meaner lives than the blacks I knew. I had no idea that I had outgrown childhood's protection until I arrived back in Stamps.

Momma took my son in one arm and folded the other around me. She held us for one sweet crushing moment. "Praise God Almighty you're home safe."

She was already moving away to keep her crying private.

"Turned into a little lady. Sure did." My Uncle Willie examined me with his quiet eyes and reached for the baby. "Let's see what you've got there."

He had been crippled in early childhood, and his affliction was never mentioned. The right side of his body had undergone severe paralysis, but his left arm and hand were huge and powerful. I laid the baby in the bend of his good arm.

"Hello, baby. Hello. Ain't he sweet?" The words slurred over his tongue and out of the numb lips. "Here, take him." His healthy muscles were too strong for a year-old wriggler.

Momma called from the kitchen, "Sister, I made you a little something to eat."

We were in the Store; I had grown up in its stronghold. Just seeing the shelves loaded with weenie sausages and Brown Plug chewing tobacco, salmon and mackerel and sardines all in their old places softened my heart and tears stood at the ready just behind my lids. But the kitchen, where Momma with her great height bent to pull cakes from the wood-burning stove and arrange the familiar food on well-known plates, erased my control and the tears slipped out and down my face to plop onto the baby's blanket.

The hills of San Francisco, the palm trees of San Diego, prostitution and lesbians and the throat hurting of Curly's departure disappeared into a never-could-have-happened land. I was home.

"Now what you crying for?" Momma wouldn't look at me for fear my tears might occasion her own. "Give the baby to me, and you go wash your hands. I'm going to make him a sugar tit. You can set the table. Reckon you remember where everything is."

The baby went to her without a struggle and she talked to him without the cooing most people use with small children. "Man. Just a little man, ain't you? I'm going to call you Man and that's that."

Momma and Uncle Willie hadn't changed. She still spoke softly and her voice had a little song in it.

"Bless my soul, Sister, you come stepping up here looking like your daddy for the world."

Christ and Church were still the pillars of her life.

"The Lord my God is a rock in a weary land. He is a great God. Brought you home, all in one piece. Praise His name."

She was, as ever, the matriarch. "I never did want you children to go to California. Too fast that life up yonder. But then, you all's their children, and I didn't want nothing to happen to you, while you're in my care. Jew was getting a little too big for his britches."

Five years before, my brother had seen the body of a black man pulled from the river. The cause of death had not been broadcast, but Bailey (Jew was short for Junior) had seen that the man's genitals had been cut away. The shock caused him to ask questions that were dangerous for a black boy in 1940 Arkansas. Momma decided we'd both be better off in California where lynchings were unheard of and a bright young

Negro boy could go places. And even his sister might find a niche for herself.

Despite the sarcastic remarks of Northerners, who don't know the region (read Easterners, Westerners, North East- erners, North Westerners, Midwesterners), the South of the United States can be so impellingly beautiful that sophisti- cated creature comforts diminish in importance.

For four days I waited on the curious in the Store, and let them look me over. I was that rarity, a Stamps girl who had gone to the fabled California and returned. I could be forgiven a few siditty airs. In fact, a pretension to worldliness was expected of me, and I was too happy to disappoint.

When Momma wasn't around, I stood with one hand on my hip and my head cocked to one side and spoke of the won- ders of the West and the joy of being free. Any listener could have asked me: if things were so grand in San Francisco, what had brought me back to a dusty mote of Arkansas? No one asked, because they all needed to believe that a land existed somewhere, even beyond the Northern Star, where Negroes were treated as people and whites were not the all-powerful ogres of their experience.

For the first time the farmers acknowledged my maturity. They didn't order me back and forth along the shelves but found subtler ways to make their wants known.

"You all have any long-grain rice, Sister?"

The hundred-pound sack of rice sat squidged down in full view.

"Yes, ma'am, I believe we do."

"Well then, I'll thank you for two pounds."

"Two pounds? Yes, ma'am."

I had seen the formality of black adult equals all my youth but had never considered that a time would come when I, too, could participate. The customs are as formalized as an eighteenth-century minuet, and a child at the race's knee learns the moves and twirls by osmosis and observation.

Values among Southern rural blacks are not quite the same as those existing elsewhere. Age has more worth than wealth, and religious piety more value than beauty.

There were no sly looks over my fatherless child. No cutting insinuations kept me shut away from the community. Knowing how closely my grandmother's friends hewed to the Bible, I was surprised not to be asked to confess my evil ways and repent. Instead, I was seen in the sad light which had been shared and was to be shared by black girls in every state in the country. I was young, yes, unmarried, yes—but I was a mother, and that placed me nearer to the people.

I was flattered to receive such acceptance from my betters (seniors) and strove mightily to show myself worthy.

Momma and Uncle Willie noted my inclusion into the adult stratum, and on my fourth day they put up no resistance when I said I was going for a night on the town. Since they knew Stamps, they knew that any carousing I chose to do would be severely limited. There was only one "joint" and the owner was a friend of theirs.

Age and travel had certainly broadened me and obviously made me more attractive. A few girls and boys with whom I'd had only generalities in common, all my life, asked me along for an evening at Willie Williams' café. The girls were going off soon to Arkansas Mechanical and Technical College to study Home Economics and the boys would be leaving for Tuskegee Institute in Alabama to learn how to farm. Although I had no education, my California past and having a baby made me equal to an evening with them.

When my escorts walked into the darkened Store,

Momma came from the kitchen, still wearing her apron, and joined Uncle Willie behind the counter.

"Evening, Mrs. Henderson. Evening, Mr. Willie."

"Good evening, children." Momma gathered herself into immobility.

Uncle Willie leaned against the wall. "Evening, Philomena, and Harriet and Johnny Boy and Louis. How you all this evening?"

Just by placing their big still bodies in the Store at that precise time, my grandmother and uncle were saying, "Be good. Be very very good. Somebody is watching you."

We squirmed and grinned and understood.

The music reached out for us when we approached the halfway point. A dark throbbing bass line whonked on the air lanes, and our bodies moved to tempo. The steel guitar urged the singer to complain

> "Well, I ain't got no
> special reason here.
> No, I ain't got no
> special reason here.
> I'm going leave
> 'cause I don't feel welcome here . . ."

THE Dew Drop In café was a dark square outline, and on its wooden exterior, tin posters of grinning white women divinely suggested Coca-Cola, R.C. Cola and Dr Pepper for complete happiness. Inside the one-room building, blue bulbs hung down precariously close to dancing couples, and the air moved heavily like stagnant water.

Our entrance was noted but no one came rushing over to welcome me or ask questions. That would come, I knew, but certain formalities had first to be observed. We all ordered Coca-Cola, and a pint bottle of sloe gin appeared by magic. The music entered my body and raced along my veins with the third syrupy drink. Hurray, I was having a good time. I had never had the chance to learn the delicate art of flirtation, so now I mimicked the other girls at the table. Fluttering one hand over my mouth, while laughing as hard as I could. The other hand waved somewhere up and to my left as if I and it had nothing to do with each other.

"Marguerite?"

I looked around the table and was surprised that everyone was gone. I had no idea how long I had sat there laughing and smirking behind my hand. I decided they had joined the dancing throng and looked up to search for my, by now, close but missing friends.

"Marguerite." L.C. Smith's face hung above me like the head of a bodyless brown ghost.

"L.C., how are you?" I hadn't seen him since my return, and as I waited for his answer a wave of memory crashed in my brain. He was the boy who had lived on the hill behind the school who rode his own horse and at fifteen picked as much cotton as the grown men. Despite his good looks he was never popular. He didn't talk unless forced. His mother had died when he was a baby, and his father drank moonshine, even during the week. The girls said he was womanish, and the boys that he was funny that way.

I commenced to giggle and flutter and he took my hand.

"Come on. Let's dance."

I agreed and caught the edge of the table to stand. Half erect, I noticed that the building moved. It rippled and buckled as if a nest of snakes were mating beneath the floors. I was concerned, but the sloe gin had numbed my brain and I couldn't panic. I held on to the table and L.C.'s hand, and tried to straighten myself up.

"Sit down. I'll be right back." He took his hand away and I plopped back into the chair. Sometime later he was back with a glass of water.

"Come on. Get up." His voice was raspy like old corn shucks. I set my intention on getting up and pressed against the iron which had settled in my thighs.

"We're going to dance?" My words were thick and cumbersome and didn't want to leave my mouth.

"Come on." He gave me his hand and I stumbled up and against him and he guided me to the door.

Outside, the air was only a little darker and a little cooler, but it cleared one corner of my brain. We were walking in the moist dirt along the pond, and the café was again a distant outline. With soberness came a concern for my virtue. Maybe he wasn't what they said.

"What are you going to do?" I stopped and faced him, readying myself for his appeal.

"It's not me. It's you. You're going to throw up." He spoke slowly. "You're going to put your finger down your throat and tickle, then you can puke."

With his intentions clear, I regained my pose.

"But I don't want to throw up. I'm not in the least—"

He closed a hand on my shoulder and shook me a little. "I say, put your finger in your throat and get that mess out of your stomach."

I became indignant. How could he, a peasant, a nobody, presume to lecture me? I snatched my shoulder away.

"Really, I'm fine. I think I'll join my friends," I said and turned toward the café.

"Marguerite." It was no louder than his earlier tone but had more force than his hand.

"Yes?" I had been stopped.

"They're not your friends. They're laughing at you." He had misjudged. They couldn't be laughing at me. Not with my sophistication and city ways.

"Are you crazy?" I sounded like a San Francisco-born debutante.

"No. You're funny to them. You got away. And then you came back. What for? And with what to show for your travels?" His tone was as soft as the Southern night and the pond lapping. "You come back swaggering and bragging that you've just been to paradise and you're wearing the very clothes everybody here wants to get rid of."

I hadn't stopped to think that while loud-flowered skirts and embroidered white blouses caused a few eyebrows to be raised in San Diego, in Stamps they formed the bulk of most girl's wardrobes.

L.C. went on, "They're saying you must be crazy. Even people in Texarkana dress better than you do. And you've been all the way to California. They want to see you show your butt outright. So they gave you extra drinks of sloe gin."

He stopped for a second, then asked, "You don't drink, do you?"

"No." He had sobered me.

"Go on, throw up. I brought some water so you can rinse your mouth after."

He stepped away as I began to gag. The bitter strong fluid gurgled out of my throat, burning my tongue. And the thought of nausea brought on new and stronger contractions.

After the cool water we walked back past the joint, and the music, still heavy, throbbed like gongs in my head. He left the glass by the porch and steered me in the direction of the Store.

His analysis had confused me and I couldn't understand why I should be the scapegoat.

He said, "They want to be free, free from this town, and crackers, and farming, and yes-sirring and no-sirring. You never were very friendly, so if you hadn't gone anywhere, they wouldn't have liked you any more. I was born here, and will die here, and they've never liked me." He was resigned and without obvious sorrow.

"But, L.C., why don't you get away?"

"And what would my poppa do? I'm all he's got." He stopped me before I could answer, and went on, "Sometimes I bring home my salary and he drinks it up before I can buy food for the week. Your grandmother knows. She lets me have credit all the time."

We were nearing the Store and he kept talking as if I weren't there. I knew for sure that he was going to continue talking to himself after I was safely in my bed.

"I've thought about going to New Orleans or Dallas, but all I know is how to chop cotton, pick cotton and hoe potatoes. Even if I could save the money to take Poppa with me, where would I get work in the city? That's what happened to him, you know? After my mother died he wanted to leave the house, but where could he go? Sometimes when he's drunk two bottles of White Lightning, he talks to her. " 'Reenie, I can see you standing there. How come you didn't take me with you, Reenie? I ain't got no place to go, Reenie. I want to be with you, Reenie.' And I act like I don't even hear him."

We had reached the back door of the Store. He held out his hand.

"Here, chew these Sen-sen. Sister Henderson ought not know you've been drinking. Good night, Marguerite. Take it easy."

And he melted into the darker darkness. The following year I heard that he had blown his brains out with a shotgun on the day of his father's funeral.

CHAPTER 17

THE midmorning sun was deceitfully mild and the wind had no weight on my skin. Arkansas summer mornings have a feathering effect on stone reality.

After five days in the South my quick speech had begun to drag, and the clipped California diction (clipped in comparison) had started to slur. I had to brace myself properly to "go downtown." In San Francisco, women dressed particularly to shop in the Geary and Market streets' big-windowed stores. Short white gloves were as essential a part of the shopping attire as girdles, which denied cleaved buttocks, and deodorant, which permitted odorless walkings up and down the steep hills.

I dressed San Francisco style for the nearly three-mile walk and proceeded through the black part of town, past the Christian Methodist Episcopal and African Methodist Episcopal churches and the proud little houses that sat above their rose bushes in grassless front yards, on toward the pond and the railroad tracks which separated white town from black town. My postwar Vinylite high heels, which were see-through plastic, crunched two inches into the resisting gravel, and I tugged my gloves all the way up to my wrist. I had won over the near-tropical inertia, and the sprightly walk, made a bit jerky by the small grabbing stones, the neat attire and the high headed position, was bound to teach the black women watching behind lace curtains how they should approach a day's downtown shopping. It would prove to the idle white women, once I reached their territory, that I knew how things should be done. And if I knew, well, didn't that mean that there were legions of Black women in other parts of the world who knew also? Up went the Black Status.

When I glided and pulled into White Town, there was a vacuum. The air had died and fallen down heavily. I looked at the white windows expecting to see curtains lose strained positions and resume their natural places. But the curtains on both sides of the street remained fixed. Then I realized that the white women were missing my halting but definitely elegant advance on their town. I then admitted my weariness, but urged my head higher and my shoulders squarer than before.

What Stamps' General Merchandise Store missed in class it made up in variety. Cheap grades of thread and chicken feed, farming implements and hair ribbons, fertilizer, shampoo, women's underwear, and B.V.D.s Socks, face powder, school supplies and belly-wrenching laxatives were shoved on and under the shelves.

I pitied the poor storekeeper and the shop attendants. When I thought of the wide aisles of San Francisco's Emporium and the nearly heard, quiet conversations in the expensive City of Paris, I gave the store a patronizing smile.

A young, very blond woman's mournful countenance met me in the middle of a crowded aisle. I gave her, "Good morning," and let a benign smile lift the corners of my lips.

"What can I do for you?" The thin face nodded at me like a sharp ax descending slowly. I thought, "The poor shabby dear." She didn't even form her words. Her question floated out like a hillbilly song, "Whakin I dew fer yew?"

"I'd like a Simplicity pattern, please." I could afford to be courteous. I was the sophisticate. When I gave her the pattern number out of my head and saw her start at my Western accent, regained for the moment, I felt a rush of kindness for the sorrowful cracker girl. I added, "If you please."

She walked behind a counter and riffled through a few aging sewing patterns, her shoulders rounding over the drawer as if its contents were in danger. Although she was twenty, or more likely eighteen, her stance and face spoke of an early surrender to the poverty of poor-white Southern life. There was no promise of sex in her hip span, nor flight in her thin short fingers.

"We ain't got it here. But I can put in a order to Texarkana for it for you."

She never looked up and spoke of the meager town twenty-five miles away as if she meant Istanbul.

"I would so much appreciate that." I did feel grateful and even more magnanimous.

"It'll be back in three days. You come in on Friday."

I wrote my name, Marguerite A. Johnson, without flourishes on the small pad she handed me, smiled encouragement to her and walked back into the now-serious noon sunshine. The heat had rendered the roads empty of pedestrians, and it assaulted my shoulders and the top of my head as if it had been lying in wait for me.

The memory of the insensate clerk prodded me into exaggerated awareness and dignity. I had to walk home at the same sprightly clip, my arms were obliged to swing in their same rhythm, and I would not under any circumstances favor the shade trees which lined the road. My head blurred with deep pains, and the rocky path swam around me, but I kept my mind keen on the propriety of my position and finally gained the Store.

Momma asked from the cool, dark kitchen, "What'd you buy, Sister?"

I swallowed the heat-induced nausea and answered, "Nothing, Momma."

THE days eased themselves around our lives like visitors in a sickroom. I hardly noticed their coming and going. Momma was as engrossed as she'd allow herself in the wonder of my son. Patting, stroking, she talked to him and never introduced in her deep voice the false humor adults tend to offer babies. He, in turn, surrendered to her. Following her from kitchen to porch to store to the backyard.

Their togetherness came to be expected. The tall and large dark-brown woman (whose movement never seemed to start or stop) was trailed one step by the pudgy little butter-yellow baby lurching, falling, now getting himself up, at moments rocking on bowed legs, then off again in the wave of Momma. I never saw her turn or stop to right him, but she would slow her march and resume when he was steady again.

My pattern had arrived from old exotic Texarkana. And I dressed for the trek downtown, and checked my hair, which was straightened to within an inch of its life and greased to desperation. From within the Store, I felt the threat of the sun but walked out into the road impelled by missionary zeal.

By the time I reached the pond and Mr. Willie Williams'

Dew Drop In, the plastic seemed to have melted to the exact shape of my feet, and sweat had popped through the quarter inch of Arrid in my armpits.

Mr. Williams served me a cold drink. "What you trying to do? Fry your brains?"

"I'm on my way to the General Merchandise Store. To pick up an order."

His smile was a two-line checkerboard of white and gold. "Be careful they don't pick you up. This sun ain't playing."

Arrogance and stupidity nudged me out of the little café and back on the white hot clay. I drifted under the shade trees, my face a mask of indifference. The skin of my thighs scudded like wet rubber as I walked deliberately by the alien white houses and on to my destination.

In the store the air lay heavily on the blades of two sluggish overhead fans, and a sweet, thick odor enveloped me at the cosmetic counter. Still, I was prepared to wander the aisles until the sun forgave our sins and withdrew its vengeance.

A tall saleswoman wearing a clerk's smock confronted me. I tried to make room for her in the narrow corridor. I moved to my left, she moved to her right. I right, she left, we jockeyed a moment's embarrassment and I smiled. Her long face answered with a smile. "You stand still and I'll pass you." It was not a request for cooperation. The hard mountain voice gave me an order.

To whom did she think she was speaking? Couldn't she see from my still-white though dusty gloves, my starched clothes, that I wasn't a servant to be ordered around? I had walked nearly three miles under a sun on fire and was neither gasping nor panting, but standing with the cool decorum of a great lady in the tacky, putrid store. She should have considered that.

"No, you stand still and I'll pass around you," I commanded.

The amazement which leaped upon her face was quickly pushed aside by anger. "What's your name? Where you from?"

A repetition of "You stand still and I'll pass around you" was ready on my tongue, when the pale woman who had taken my order slack-butted down the aisle toward us. The familiar face brought back the sympathy I had felt for her and I explained the tall woman into limbo with "Excuse me, here comes my salesgirl."

The dark-haired woman turned quickly and saw her colleague approach. She put herself between us, and her voice rasped out in the quiet store: "Who is this?"

Her head jerked back to indicate me. "Is this that sassy Ruby Lee you was telling me about?"

The clerk lifted her chin and glanced at me, then swirled to the older woman. "Naw, this ain't her." She flipped the pages of a pad in her hand and continued, "This one's Margaret or Marjorie or something like that."

Her head eased up again and she looked across centuries at me. "How do you pronounce your name, gal? Speak up."

In that moment I became rootless, nameless, pastless. The two white blurs buoyed before me.

"Speak up," she said. "What's your name?"

I clenched my reason and forced their faces into focus. "My name"—here I drew myself up through the unrevenged slavery—"is Miss Johnson. If you have occasion to use my name, which I seriously doubt, I advise you to address me as Miss Johnson. For if I need to allude to your pitiful selves, I shall call you Miss Idiot, Miss Stupid, Miss Fool or whatever name a luckless fate has dumped upon you."

The women became remote even as I watched them. They seemed actually to float away from me down the aisle; and from watching their distant faces, I knew they were having trouble believing in the fact of me.

"And where I'm from is no concern of yours, but rather where you're going. I'll slap you into the middle of next week if you even dare to open your mouths again. Now, take that filthy pattern and stick it you-know-where."

As I strode between the two women I was sheathed in satisfaction. There had been so few critical times when my actions met my approval that now I congratulated myself. I had got them told and told correctly. I pictured the two women's mouths still open in amazement. The road was less rocky and the sun's strength was weakened by my pleasure. Congratulations were in order.

There was no need to stop at Mr. Williams' for a refreshing drink. I was as cool as a fountain inside as I headed home.

Momma stood on the porch facing the road. Her arms hung at her sides and she made no motions with her head. Yet something was wrong. Tension had distorted the statue straightness and caused her to lean leftward. I stopped patting myself on the back and ran to the Store.

When I reached the one-step porch, I looked up in her face. "Momma, what's the matter?"

Worry had forced a deep line down either side of her nostrils past her stiffly held lips.

"What's wrong?"

"Mr. Coleman's granddaughter, Miss June, just called from the General Merchandise Store." Her voice quaked a little. "She said you was downtown showing out."

So that's how they described my triumph to her. I decided

to explain and let her share in the glory. I began, "It was the principle of the thing, Momma—"

I didn't even see the hand rising, and suddenly it had swung down hard against my cheek.

"Here's your principle, young miss."

I felt the sting on my skin and the deep ache in my head. The greatest hurt was that she didn't ask to hear my side.

"Momma, it was a principle." My left ear was clogged, but I heard my own voice fuzzily.

The hand didn't surprise me the second time, but the same logic which told me I was right at the white store told me I was no less right in front of Momma. I couldn't allow myself to duck the blow. The backhand swing came down on my right cheek.

"Here's your principle." Her voice had a far-away-tunnel sound.

"It was a principle, Momma." Tears poured down my burning face, and ache backed up in my throat.

The hand came again and again each time I mumbled "principle," and I found myself in the soft dust in front of the porch. I didn't want to move. I never wanted to get up again.

She stepped off the porch and caught my arms. "Get up. Stand up, I say."

Her voice never allowed disobedience. I stood, and looked at her face. It glistened as if she had just dashed a pan of water over her head.

"You think 'cause you've been to California these crazy people won't kill you? You think them lunatic cracker boys won't try to catch you in the road and violate you? You think because of your all-fired principle some of the men won't feel like putting their white sheets on and riding over here to stir up trouble? You do, you're wrong. Ain't nothing to protect you and us except the good Lord and some miles. I packed you and the baby's things, and Brother Wilson is coming to drive you to Louisville."

That afternoon I climbed into a horse-drawn wagon, and took my baby from Momma's arms. The baby cried as we pulled away, and Momma and Uncle Wilson stood waving and crying good-bye.

CHAPTER 18

MOMMA'S intent to protect me had caused her to hit me in the face, a thing she had never done, and to send me away to where she thought I'd be safe. So again, the South and I had parted and again I was headed for the cool gray hills of San Francisco. I raged on the train that white stupidity could so dictate my movements and looked unsheathed daggers at every white face I saw.

If the tables could have turned at that instant, I would gladly have consigned every white person living and the millions dead to a hell where the devil was blacker than their fears of blackness and more cruel than forced starvation. But, powerless, I spent the time on the train entertaining the baby when I thought of it, and wondering if I would be met by a warrant for my arrest when I returned to California.

The city didn't even know I had been away, and Mother took me and the baby to a room in her new fourteen-room house as if I had just returned from a long-intended holiday.

I found a job as a short-order cook in a tiny greasy spoon. The men who ate there were defeated leftovers from the now-closed war plants. They slouched into the fifth-rate dingy diner hugging their distress.

The job paid very little and the atmosphere of despair that never lifted depressed me. I left the restaurant each afternoon feeling that the rancid cooking oil and the old men's sadness had seeped into my pores and were crawling through my body.

One afternoon I went into a record shop across the street from the diner and found a woman who was friendly and warm behind the counter. She was white and thirtyish, and didn't condescend to either my color or my youth. When I told her that I liked blues, she pulled out some old Columbia Blue Labels. I said that I also liked jazz, and she suggested recent Charlie "Bird" Parker releases. I let the music wash away the odors and moods of the restaurant, and I left the shop with more records than I could afford. I had agreed with her that I should start collecting the Dial records featuring Bird, Max Roach, Al Haig, Bud Powell, Dizzy Gillespie and others who she said were going to be the "masters." Each payday I kept out enough money to pay my own way at Mother's, and spent the rest on records and books.

Mother was unhappy that my job made me unhappy. She always knew her "daughter had great potential" and was determined that if she had anything to do with it, I was going to realize it.

Weeks later she and I sat in the dining room and picked and poked through the classifieds for my future.

I was nearly nineteen, had a baby, responsibilities and no real profession. I could cook Creole and was a fast, friendly cocktail waitress. Also I was qualified as an absentee madam, but I somehow felt that I simply had not yet "found out my niche" (I had just discovered that phrase and yo-yo'ed it around with frequent and gay abandon).

"Private secretary. If you could type fast enough and do shorthand." Mother was serious. Her pretty face was lined with concentration. "Telephone operator, pays pretty good."

I reminded her that we'd already been through that.

"Key punch. Stenographer. You need training, baby."

She looked at me spot on and added, "Anything worth doing is worth doing well."

I didn't dare remind her that everything I had done had been well done.

"What is Alice doing? What about Jean Mae, and the twins? What are they all doing? Going to college?" Her voice and round black eyes worried me for answers.

Jean Mae, the neighborhood's sepia Betty Grable, had a job hopping cars at a popular drive-in. I hardly had the face, figure or sexuality to be taken in at that restaurant. Alice could be seen nightly whistling down Post Street and up Sutter, her young walk exaggerated, her thin voice insinuating the lone sailor into following three paces behind her to the nearest transient hotel.

The twins married twins, which seemed as appalling to me as streetwalking. I felt there was a closet incest about the whole thing.

The small percentage of classmates who went on to college had become unbearably stuck-up and boring. So I found no inspiration among my peers.

"Companion, Chauffeurette." That I could do. I immediately set a film to flickering on my mind screen. In a snappy uniform, no cap, gray serge and British walker shoes, I drove a man around who was the spitting image of Lionel Barrymore.

He always addressed me as "Johnson" and while we liked and respected each other, we took pains never to show it. Late nights, he would call me into the drawing room and I would stand at attention, easily.

"Johnson. Tomorrow's a beaut."

"Yes, sir?"

"We go up to the city, then back to the country club, then the city, then the farm. A little hard on you, I fear."

"It's my job, sir."

"I could count on you to say that, Johnson."

"Yes, sir."

"Good night."

"Good night, sir."

Mother's gaze followed her ringed fingers up and down the page.

"You'd have to live in and it doesn't really pay enough for you to afford a full-time baby-sitter." She flipped the paper closed.

"Take anything that looks like something. You can always quit. Or there's a chance that you won't rise to the challenge and you'll be fired. But the only thing to remember is that 'you were looking for a job when you found that one.' So whoever fires you ain't getting no cherry." She got up and went into the kitchen.

"How about a Dubonnet"—ice already clucked against the sides of glasses—"with a twist of lemon? I'm going to fix myself a Scotch."

When I was around ten in Arkansas, I saw a glamorous actress play a jaunty chauffeurette in a movie. She maneuvered an Oldsmobile with one hand and was as chic as a model. I looked at the paper again and thought about the chauffeuring job. A wisp of nostalgia floated in my heart. The uniform, the easy camaraderie with the staff, the asexuality with my boss, and peace. Just like the Army. Routine, honorable work, hail-fellows well met, good-hearted companions and fair-minded officers. The Army! Just the thing. The idea snap-saluted in my brain. The Army!

I bounded into the kitchen and nearly collided with Mother and her tray of gold and purple drinks. I had developed some grace, quite a lot when I kept my mind on being graceful, but in unguarded moments my body tended to respond giraffe-like to stimuli.

"Mother!" She had righted the threatened glasses and pushed past me for the dining room. "I'm going in the Army!"

She set down the Dubonnet. "You as a sergeant and the baby as a private?"

Her tongue was sharper than the creases in zoot pants and I knew better than to try to best her. I said nothing.

"What would be the value of becoming a WAC?" she asked.

"The Army has all those side benefits and I could learn a trade. There's the G.I. Bill, and when you get out you can go back to school and buy a home at the same time."

"Side benefits" had caused a glint in Mother's eyes.

"Now"—she pushed the wine toward me—"now you have to consider if you're serious. Because if you are, it would be like volunteering for jail. People tell you when to sleep, eat, wake up, work. Personally, I couldn't do it in a million years." Her face frowned revulsion. "But in a way the country would be helping you get a start in life."

Behind her smooth beige forehead, deep thoughts were being turned over, examined and replaced or discarded.

"If you are serious and get in, we'll talk to Mrs. Peabody

about taking care of the baby. You could sign up for a two-year tour, save your money, and study languages and advanced typing."

She was talking my future into shape.

"Try out for Officer Candidate School or Officers' Training Corps. Nothing they could say to you but yes or no. And when you go down there, remember they need you as much as you need them." She saw my disbelief and explained "The U.S. Army needs nice colored girls, well raised from good families. That's what I meant." She reached for her lipstick tube (never far away). "Government is going to give you an education and a start in life and you're going to give class to that uniform."

"Mother, they would examine me, physically, and find out about the baby."

"You don't have stretch marks and because you breast-fed, your breasts never got out of shape." Her words nudged past indifference. "That's not what you ought to be thinking of. No. Decide if you want the Army for two years. Away from your baby and family. Taking orders, and keeping your temper under wraps. That's a decision no one can make for you nor help you make."

She got up from the table and visited one of her flashiest smiles on me.

"I have a date now. We can talk more when you're ready. Remember if you decide for the Army, I'll support you. If you decide to be a whore, all I can say is, be the best. Don't be a funky chippie. Go with class."

She pasted a waxy kiss on my forehead and draped her Kolinsky over her shoulders.

"How do I look?"

"Beautiful."

She tugged the furs into a more casual drape and laughed. "You only say it 'cause it's true."

Her high heels tapped toward the door in drumming rhythm.

CHAPTER 19

———————— 〰️ ————————

THE U.S. Recruitment Center hadn't tried hard. The offices were at the foot of San Francisco's Market Street, near the glamorous Ferry Building, but none of the latter's exotica strayed to the prefab whitewash walls of the Center.

A uniformed woman offered me a Dagwood sandwich of brochures and applications and I sat down to read.

Indeed, it sounded like what I needed. Food, shelter, training and comradeship. Two years and I could buy a house for myself and my son. Might find a man, too. After all, there was a conglomeration of men in the Army. All I had to do now was maneuver between outrageous lies and delicate untruths to pass the various tests. (I wasn't concerned about the I.Q., but about the Rorschach.) Had I just wanted to join the regular Women's Army it would have taxed my creative lying skills, but I had gone one further. Mother had said, "Start at the top," so I decided to try out for Officer Candidate School. I thought daily trips to the Center would help my case.

The war's end had left the skeletal WAC staff with little to do except file papers in triplicate and dress up in privilege.

For nearly a month I provided diversion. Naturally, the clerks couldn't enjoy my artful dodging as much as I, because they weren't privy to my secrets.

I sidled over the questionnaires and applications, double-checking, doubly-lying. Married . . . check one. No. Children . . . check one. No.

My cavorting brain was of no use to me at the medical examination, though. There the doctors opened my mouth wide (I needed dental work; the Army would pay), thudded and tapped and listened to my strong lungs and courageous heart. All was well.

The gynecologist's table was my Armageddon. There on the cold table, gray steel instruments would probe between my legs and into the unknown territory where my deepest guilts had lodged. I had no more idea of the construction of a woman's regenerative organs than I had of the structure of the moon. Surely, I thought, there would be some scars visible from my son's birth. Some leftover tube hanging down which would signal to the knowledgeable that I was a mother and therefore unfit to serve my country (which by this time I had come to love with a maudlin sentimentality).

"We'll take a few slides." The nurse's face was stony, and the doctor ignored my face, acting as if I was nothing but a thin chest, flat belly and long black legs.

I asked why.

"These are venereal-disease tests." She spoke as if she were weather-watching. I'd gladly have settled for syphilis and gonorrhea. If the Army could take care of my teeth, a couple of injections would cure the diseases.

"The tests will be back in a few days."

I tried to scrape from their faces any information they had gathered. But those faces were trained in suppression. I wanted to shout at their closed ears, "I'll wait. I'll sit in the outer office and wait for the results." But I too had some training—that is, "Never let white folks know what you really think. If you're sad, laugh. If you're bleeding inside, dance."

"I'll be away for a few days," I lied, "but I'll phone as soon as I return." I tried to make it sound as if I would be doing them a favor.

Three or four days jittered by with no pretense at flowing, and then the phone call came.

"Miss Johnson?" I recognized the voice with echoes of starched uniforms and drill squadrons.

"Yes, I'm Miss Johnson." I tried to put "I'm Miss Johnson, so what?" into my own response and failed.

"Sergeant Matthews at the Induction Center."

I know. I know. Go on, dammit.

"I'm calling to tell you you've passed all your tests and have been included in the March-April quota of personnel to enter Office Candidate School. Is that all right with you?"

I suddenly had dirigible-sized air pockets in my cheeks which prevented me from making any sound except a loud explosion. I nodded into the telephone.

"Will you be prepared to leave the San Francisco area at the beginning of May for Fort Lee, Virginia?"

The air plopped out of my mouth and I jerked the phone away. God knows I didn't want to frighten the sergeant and give her a reason to re-examine my dossier of lies. I turned the sound into a fake cough and brought the mouthpiece back.

"Excuse me. A little spring cough. Oh yes, I can certainly be ready for May first." I was in a little more control, so I added, "I'm most happy to have this opportunity to serve my country and I shall—"

She interrupted, "Yes, well, come down in the next few days and sign the loyalty oath. Good-bye." And hung up.

Now I was ready. Things had arranged themselves in my favor at last. For the next two years I would have the security of purpose and the dignity of being a soldier in good standing in the Army of the United States of America.

Natural restraint and the conceit of sophistication kept me from rushing down immediately to sign the loyalty oath. I was able to keep myself away for two days before I surrendered.

I stood in front of the flag, one hand on the Bible, the other clasped to my breast, and swore I would defend this land from her enemies, etc., etc. The deep motives, the noble intent so moved me that with the least encouragement I would have dissolved in a flood of patriotic tears.

Mother was happy but not surprised at my success story. When I told Bailey that I would soon be going into the Army, he turned a cold stare on me and asked without relishing curiosity, "What the shit for? Men are trying like hell to get out and my sister is dying to get in. You dumb bunny." The air between Bailey and me had coarsened with our growing up and thickened with his cynicism. He could no longer see me clearly and I could not distinguish his black male disappointment in life.

It could not be said that Bailey was living at home, but more accurately that he was based there. He worked as a waiter on the Southern Pacific trains running from San Francisco to Chicago or Los Angeles or Houston.

Few black families are without ties to the U.S. railroads. The early-twentieth-century Negro aristocrats were the families of ministers, morticians, teachers and railroad men. Passes to ride the trains were traded in Southern black areas as easily as legitimate money. And many poor black families ate their beans and greens from good china and used heavy silver from the Union Pacific, Southern Pacific and New York Central.

Bailey was still the plum pretty black color and his teeth shone white like promises. His hair was glossy and his small hands delicate and graceful. But all the gentle reminders of his love for me through our childhood stopped at his eyes. It seemed some confrontation, which he had kept secret, dulled their shine and left them flat and unseeing.

His fast speech, which used to stumble into a stutter with excitement, had slowed, and a songless monotone rasped out his meanings. When he was home from a trip, he never sat around with Mother and me, playing pinochle or coon can, as we used to do, but hurriedly put down his gear and left the house for some mysterious destination. He successfully blocked my prying by saying, "Take care of yourself and your baby and your own business and that'll take all your time."

When I tried to involve Mother in discussion of his whereabouts and how abouts, she said nearly the same thing but generally added, "He's a man. He's got a job and his health and strength. Some people have to make it through life with less." And that was that.

Papa Ford, who had been brought to the new house, sat bowed over his coffee in the warm kitchen.

I asked him, "Papa, what's Bailey doing? Why is he changing so?"

He lifted his head and relished a toothless mouth. Smack. Smack.

"Uh. Uh, girl. Uh, uh." He lowered his head, loving the doom he hinted.

"Papa, what does that mean? Say something."

The passage of years had ground away his emotional-transition apparatus. He would often shift in a moment from a dozing indifference to a fighting fury. He did so then.

"Don't ask so many goddam questions. Keep your goddam big eyes open. You're no shitty-ass baby." A slurp from his mug and he was nearly asleep again.

CHAPTER 20

———————— ❧ ————————

I HAD to make arrangements for my personal belongings. I told mother that when I got out of the Army I would dress in suits, and my cashmere-sweater sets would match kick-pleated Scotch-plaid skirts. I wouldn't be needing the old clothes. Mother had decided they were good enough to be given to charity. I remembered the large St. Vincent de Paul's trucks, backing down our driveway once a year during my teens, collecting Mother's unwanted items. After a brief but pointed sermon when Mother spoke of "those less fortunate than you," I chose the Salvation Army as my beneficiary. Those fresh clean faces in their absurd regalia playing their uninspired music, unheeded, had always depressed me. They had to be the most deserving.

The records would stay in the house. Mother enjoyed Lester Young, Billie Holiday, Louis Jordan, Buddy Johnson and Arthur "Big Boy" Crudup as much as I. She'd play them at her parties and think of me.

I found it hard to think of leaving my books. They had

been my elevators out of the midden, and to whom could I entrust such close friends?

The benevolent act of giving away my clothes, however, spilled over into that decision making. Hospitals were the answer. I was certain that lean and lonely tubercular patients would have their spirits lifted reading the *Topper* stories of Thorne Smith, and I had proved it possible to read Robert Benchley's essays and short stories over a hundred times and still laugh. Ann Petry's *The Street*, all Thomas Wolfe, Richard Wright and Hemingway would be given to an old-folks home. But the Russian writers would be packed away in mothballs and stored in our basement. I would savor the idea of Dostoevsky's, Tolstoy's and Gorki's volumes molding in the dank cellar, wisps of camphor and odors of wet earth floating above them.

I quit my job to spend more time with Guy, to record his cherubic smile and be amazed at the beauty of his coordination. He seldom cried and seemed a budding introvert, for although he never thrust himself from company, he appeared to be equally amused alone. A baby's love for his mother is probably the sweetest emotion we can savor. When my son heard my voice at the downstairs door he'd begin to sing, and when I arrived in his view he'd fall back on his fat legs, his behind would thud to the floor and he'd laugh, his big head rocking up and down.

I knew it would be hard to leave him. Hard on me, but harder on him, for he had no way of understanding that I was gone to prepare a place for us. I hugged his sweetness to me and squeezed my love into his pores. If we were to have a decent life, a small but neat house, good neighborhood and schools, bulky knit sweaters and the expensive tennis shoes I saw large boys wearing, I'd have to get some kind of training and I needed help. Uncle Sam was going to be more a friend to me than any of my bad blood uncles.

With my clothes gone to the Salvation Army and my books packed in wooden boxes downstairs, I spent my remaining time gazing at the training manual and familiarizing myself with creases and salutes and drill formations, how a bunk should be made and how officers were to be addressed.

A week before I was to be inducted, a military voice over the telephone ordered me down to the Recruitment Center.

"I can come this morning or this afternoon."

"This morning! And that's an order, soldier."

"It sounds urgent." Maybe our departure date had been moved up.

"It's more urgent than that. It's about some discrepancy on your documents. We'll see you this morning." Click.

Dammit, dammit and double damn. Probably some ruthless, relentless doctor had re-examined my charts and found that I'd had a baby. And I had sworn that everything I had written was God's own truth. There were laws to punish criminals who lied ("perjury" it was called) on oath. And it must have been worse to lie on oath *and* the flag.

Mother had taken Guy out for the morning, to leave me alone with my army books. I had no one to accompany me. I dressed as I wondered. I shook as I planned. It was pretty certain I wasn't going into the Army, but I might go to jail if the Army wanted to press charges. I should have known better than to lie to the government. People always said Uncle Sam would spend a thousand dollars to get you if you stole a three-cent stamp from him. He was more revengful than God.

I couldn't run. I couldn't hide. I went to the government building.

On the bus I soft-conned myself. I had done so well on the examinations that if I came clean and explained that I had made solid arrangements for my son's care for two years, they might make an exception. It could be simple, if only I got a kind interviewer and could stop shaking.

"Marguerite Johnson?"

The woman's long thin neck rose out of wide sloping shoulders and her voice skidded like a fire alarm. I would have liked her face softer.

"Yes." Er . . . "Yes, ma'am." She was an officer. Oh hell, I mean . . . "Yes, sir."

"Did you or did you not sign the loyalty oath?"

"I did." Did I? I had gone down a few weeks before and sworn to uphold the flag, defend the country and protect my fellow Americans with my life, if need be. I had been so moved by my sincerity that I added to myself, "My country may she always be right but right or wrong, my country." Off we go into the wild blue yonder and the caissons go rolling along.

"Were you or were you not asked if you had ever been a member of the Communist party?"

"I was asked, and I said no." Well, if that was all it was! I felt the blood pushing to open up its old passages and start to flow again.

"You lied, Johnson." The voice sirened up to a screech.

"Lied, sir? No, sir. I've never—"

"This is your signature, Johnson?" She produced the loyalty oath by slight of hand. I didn't need to peer to see the large curving Marguerite Johnson.

"Yes, sir. That is my signature."

She flipped the paper over and grinned her pleasure. "The California Labor School is on the House Un-American Activities list, Johnson. Do you know why?"

"No, sir. I only studied dance and drama there."

"Oh, come now. Don't be stupid. It's a Communist organization and you know it."

"Maybe so, but I have never been a member."

"You went to the school for two years." She had regained her composure, her stiffness.

"But that was when I was fourteen and fifteen. I had just come from the South, and a playground teacher got me a scholarship. It was because I had trouble talking—"

"Communists are ungodly, Johnson. And this man's army fights under God."

I felt as if I were drowning in straw. The light was still visible but no amount of struggling brought me nearer to it.

"Because you were young and, I hope, you're still innocent, the Army is not going to bring charges of falsification against you. But we definitely cannot risk you as a soldier in our army, Johnson. Dismissed."

I was suspended, physically and mentally, for a second.

"Dismissed."

I know I'd have made a good soldier because without the benefit of habit or training, my body turned sharply and walked out into the sunshine.

Mother and the baby were still out when I returned to the big house. Papa Ford was away on his noonday constitutional. The rooms were all dark and cool. I sat at the ornate dining-room table and tried to sort things out.

My clothes were gone, I had no job and I had been rejected by the Army. That damn institution, which accepts everybody (to tell from its soldiers), had turned me down. My life had no center, no purpose. I had to admit, though, that I had lied. Not on the issue they charged against me (hell, I wouldn't have recognized Stalin if he'd been in my class when I was fourteen. Literally, all white folks still looked alike to me: pale and similar), but I had lied about Guy's birth. I wondered if justice was served. If maybe I should just shut up and take my punishment. I needed Bailey. I longed for the old days when I could speak to him and work out my problems.

I got up from the table and opened the door to his room. It had a strange emptiness. Not as if the occupant had just stepped out and was expected back, but as if it had never been occupied and expected nothing. There was a deadness in the air. I turned on the overhead light, went to the windows and pulled up the shades. The gray spring light dared only to enter a yard or so. I decided to change his linen, clean up and put fresh flowers in his room. Meanwhile I would think over my problem.

I stripped the blankets and folded them, then I tugged at the linen. For a moment I was so amazed I forgot my whereabouts. This couldn't be Bailey's bed. He was the model of cleanliness, neatness, decorum. Every member of my family had said at one time or other, "Maya should have been a boy and Bailey a girl. She's so sloppy and he's so neat"—and more to that effect.

The sheets were gray and black with dirt. An odor of perfumed hair oil and must lifted heavily. I tugged at the edges and let the sheets slide to the floor. The pillows rode along on the end of the sheet. As they tumbled, a small round bundle wrapped in brown paper bounced down at my feet.

I opened it without needing to. Thin brown cigarettes were held together with three rubber bands.

Even in his absence, Bailey had helped me. I lighted one of the cigarettes and in minutes was snickering over the stupidity of the Establishment. The U.S. Army with its corps of spies had been fooled by a half-educated black girl. I sat down on Bailey's bed and laughed until I had to fight for my breath.

CHAPTER 21

———————— ⟋ ————————

I TOOK a job as swing-shift waitress in a day-and-night restaurant called the Chicken Shack. The record player blared the latest hits incessantly and the late-night clientele spent their overflow energy loudly in the brightly lighted booths.

Smoking grass eased the strain for me. I made a connection at a restaurant nearby. People called it Mary Jane, hash, grass, gauge, weed, pot, and I had absolutely no fear of using it. In the black ghetto of the forties, marijuana, cocaine, hop (opium) and heroin were only a little harder to obtain than rationed whiskey. Although my mother didn't use anything but Scotch (Black & White), she often sang a song popular in the thirties that at its worst didn't condemn grass, and at its best extolled its virtues.

> Dream about a reefer five foot long
> Vitamin but not too strong
> You'll be high but not for long
> If you're a viper.

I'm the queen of everything
I got to get high before I can swing
Light some tea and let it be
If you're a viper.

Now when your throat gets dry
you know you're high
Everything is dandy
You truck on down to the candy store
And bust your conk on peppermint candy

Then you know your brown body scent
You don't give a damn if you don't pay your rent
Light some tea and let it be
If you're a viper.

I LEARNED new postures and developed new dreams. From a natural stiffness I melted into a grinning tolerance. Walking on the streets became high adventure, eating my mother's huge dinners an opulent entertainment, and playing with my son was side-cracking hilarity. For the first time, life amused me.

Positive dreaming was introduced on long, slow drags of the narcotic. I was going to do all right in the world, going to have it made—and no doubt through the good offices of a handsome man who would love me to distraction.

My charming prince was going to appear out of the blue and offer me a cornucopia of goodies. I would only have to smile to have them brought to my feet.

R.L. Poole was to prove my dreams at least partially prophetic. When I opened the door to his ring and informed him that I was Rita Johnson, his already long face depressed another inch.

"The . . . uh . . . dancer?" His voice was slow and cloudy.

Dancer? Of course. I had been a cook, waitress, madam, bus girl—why not a dancer? After all, it was the only thing I had studied.

"Yes, I'm a dancer." I looked at him boldly. "Why?"

"I'm looking for a dancer, to work with me."

I thought he might be a talent scout for a chorus line or maybe the big stage show, featuring colored dancers, called "Change Your Luck."

"Come in."

We sat at the dining-room table and I offered a coffee. He looked me over, one feature at a time. My legs (long), my hips (spare), my breasts (nearly nonexistent). He drank the coffee slowly.

"I've studied since I was fourteen," I said.

If the U.S. Army was going to penalize me for having gone to the California Labor School, it was just possible that someone else would find the time spent there valuable. I was right. His eyes moved from an examination of my body back to my face.

"I'm Poole. From Chicago." His announcement held no boast, and I was sure that represented sophistication rather than false modesty. "I do rhythm tap and I want a girl partner. She doesn't have to do much but flash. Are you agva?" ("Flash" and "A.G.V.A." were words unknown to me.)

I sat quietly and looked at him. Let him figure it out for himself.

"I met the woman at the record shop and she told me about you. Said all you talked about was dancing. She gave me your address.

"Some cats from the Local, musicians, straightened me

out with the contacts for a few gigs. Scale is twenty-two fifty, but I'll do a few under scale to get some ends together."

I hadn't the slightest notion of what he was talking about. Scale. Agva. Gigs. Local. Ends.

"More coffee?" I went into the kitchen, walking like a model, chin down and sternum up, and my tail bone tucked under like white women.

I put on a fresh pot of coffee and tried desperately to decide on a role for myself. Should I be mysterious and sultry, asking nothing, answering all questions with a knowing smirk, or should I be the open, friendly, palsy every-boy's-sister girl-next-door type? No decision came to my mind, so I went back into the dining room, my legs stuck together with fine decorum.

"What did you study?"

"Ballet. Modern Ballet and the Theory of Dance." I made it sound like Advanced Thermonuclear Propulsion.

His face fell again.

"Any tap-dancing?"

"No."

"Jazz?"

"No."

"Acrobatics?"

"No." I was losing him, so I jumped in the gap. "I used to win every jitterbug contest. I can do the Texas Hop. The Off Time. The boogie-woogie. The Camel Walk. The new Coup de Grâce. And I can do the split."

With that I stood up, straddle-legged, and looked down into his sad face, then I began to slide down to the floor.

I was unprepared for the movement (I had on a straight skirt), but R.L. was less ready than I. As my legs slipped apart and down, I lifted my arms in the graceful ballet position

number 1 and watched the impresario's face race from mild
interest to incredulous. My hem caught mid-thigh and I felt
my equilibrium teeter. With a quick slight of hand I jerked up
my skirt and continued my downward glide. I hummed a
little snatch of song during the last part of the slither, and kept
my mind on Sonja Henie in her cute little tutus.

Unfortunately, I hadn't practiced the split in months, so
my pelvic bones resisted with force. I was only two inches
from the floor, and I gave a couple of little bounces. I accomplished more than I planned. My skirt seams gave before my
bones surrendered. Then my left foot got caught between the
legs of Mother's heavy oak table, and the other foot jumped at
the gas heater and captured the pipe that ran from the jets into
the wall. Pinned down at my extremities with the tendons in
my legs screaming for ease, I felt as if I were being crucified to
the floor, but in true "show must go on" fashion I kept my
back straight and my arms uplifted in a position that would
have made Pavlova proud. Then I looked at R.L. to see what
impression I was making. Pity at my predicament was
drawing him up from his chair, and solicitude was written
over his face with a brush wider than a kitchen mop.

My independence and privacy would not allow me to
accept help. I lowered my arms and balanced my hands on the
floor and jerked my right foot. It held on to the pipe, so I
jerked again. I must have been in excellent shape. The pipe
came away from the stove, and gas hissed out steadily like ten
fat men resting on a summer's day.

R.L. stepped over me and looked down into the gas jet.
"Goddam." He swiveled over to the window and opened it as
wide as it would go, then back down to the stove. Near the
wall at the end of the pipe, he found a tap and turned it. The
hissing died and the thick sweetish odor diluted.

I had still to extricate my other leg from the avaricious table.

R.L. lifted an edge of the table, and my ankle was miraculously free. I could have gotten up, but my feelings were so hurt by the stupid clumsiness that I just rolled over on my stomach, beat my hands on the floor and cried like a baby.

There was no doubt that R.L. Poole had just witnessed his strangest audition. He could have walked down the hall and out the door, leaving me breathing in the dust of the ancient rug, but he didn't. I heard the chair creak, announcing that he had sat back down.

I was sure he was doing his best to hold in his laughter. I tried for more tears, to irritate him and force him to leave, but the tear ducts had closed and the sound I made was as false as a show girl's eyelashes. Nothing for it but to get up.

I dried my face with dusty hands and lifted my head. R.L. was sitting at the table in the same chair, his head propped up with his hand. The dark-brown face was somber and he said quietly, "Well, anyway, you've got nice legs."

When we went to a nearby rehearsal hall I was amazed to see R.L. Poole move. The wind seemed to make him dance. I pictured his lean bony legs as being attached directly to his sharp shoulders with skeletal pins. For he would hunch his shoulders and glide across the rehearsal-hall floor, his heels and toes tapping below him in a fusillade of small explosions, his arms dangling at his side, his face a pockmarked oval.

He tried to simplify the intricate tap rhythms by singing them to me in a rough, low voice. "Boom, boom, boo rah, boo rah, boo rah, boo rah, brah, brah." Sharp slaps on the floor, dust rising from the old wood.

With the polish of a professional, R.L. made it all appear easy. I telescoped my energy on the gliding steps of the flash, with no less purpose than a ballet student mastering a tour jeté. I would rise my arms shoulder-high, then open them out slowly, take two sliding steps, bend one knee and hold the position. An accomplished flash partner frames and highlights the principal dancer when he is tapping out complex rhythms. To be able to let my body swing free over the floor and the crushing failures in my past was freedom. I thanked R.L. for my liberation and fell promptly in love with him.

CHAPTER 22

————————⟨⟩————————

I COMMITTED myself to a show-business career, and dancing and studying dance swallowed me. Charlie Parker's "Cool Breeze" was my practice piece. Flash, slide through the opening riff, then stash during Bird's solo; keeping soft-shoe time by dusting the boards with the soles of my feet, then breaking during Bud Powell's piano wizardry. Break, cross step. Chicago. Fall. Fall. Break, crossover. Apple. Break. Time step. Slap crossover. Then break and Fall off the Log, going out on the closing riff.

I practiced until my ankles ached, without complaint, and was more than rewarded when R.L. told me one day, "After we break in our act out here, I think we'll go East. Big Time. Join Duke's or Basie's road show."

My concern was not how I'd manage with my son on the Big-time Circuit, but how I could perfect my flash so that R.L. wouldn't go looking for a prettier partner. I used my time at the Chicken Shack to strengthen my ankles. When I was behind the counter I stood on tiptoe, letting one heel down, then raising it, and pressing the other to the floor.

When R.L. decided we were ready to try out our act, I sprang my homemade costume on him. I had gone to a theatrical store and bought a wig, coke feathers, a padded bra and a G-string. I sewed the shiny black feathers on the scanty outfit, then added a few sequins and a little sparkle for show. My costume could be held in one balled fist, and the G-string barely covered my pubic hair and the cleavage of my buttocks.

"Er . . . no." He lowered his head and searched painfully for the words he wanted. "Uh . . . Rita . . . no. That won't . . . uh . . . get it . . . That's . . . wh . . . a shake dancer's rig . . . I mean, I'll show you . . . Something like a bathing suit . . . with spangles . . ."

I stood before him, my oiled skin gleaming, the fluffy wig trembling with ringlets on my head, withering with disappointment. My costume was a faithful copy of L'Tanya's, the popular interpretive dancer who was a current favorite at the Champagne Supper Club.

"You'll look . . . I mean, tap shoes are gonna look . . . I mean, they don't go together . . ."

I remembered. L'Tanya danced barefoot, with a string of little bells around her ankles and rings on her toes. I reluctantly agreed that my creation didn't fit a rhythm tap routine but put it away for future use.

R.L. rented a red, white and blue costume for me that was cut like a one-piece bathing suit. I added a top hat and cane, and we were ready for our first gig in a small night club down the peninsula. Ah, the smell of grease paint!

Our routine was honed to a fine point, our flashes and stashes and hand movements coordinated in machinelike precision. My costume fit passably well, my hair was done beautifully, and I had on enough makeup to stave off a winter cold.

The orchestra struck up our music and I led "Poole and Rita" out on the dance floor.

Dum dum te dum dum dum.

"And now, breaking in their new act, from way out Chicago way—Poole and Rita!"

I was miraculously in the center of an empty floor, with lights blazing down and I felt nearly naked. Just out of the glare I saw what appeared like a thousand knees and legs around small tables. I couldn't make out faces in the gloom, but I was sure they were there and probably all staring at me.

R.L. glided onto the floor, tap-tap-tapping away, flashed by me and I wanted to grab his hand. He pulled away to anywhere, but I was frozen in the spotlight.

Boom boom boom rah boom rah, boom rah brah, brah.

I realized that I was frightened and I nearly panicked. My God, what was going to happen? I'd never be able to leave this place. A stake had been driven down through my head and body, rooting me forever to this spot.

R.L. flashed by again.

Boom rah boom rah.

If he would only stop that silly tap-dancing and take my hand, we could leave.

He marched up and spoke to me under the music.

"Come on, Rita. Break. Break!"

Break what? I looked at him as if I had never seen him before.

He put his arm around my shoulder like Astaire did Rogers in one of their military parodies.

He looked at me and gave me a push that almost sent me into one of the tables, and hissed, "Break, goddammit, break!"

I broke.

I started dancing all over the place. Tapping, flashing,

stashing up and down the floor. I threw in a little Huckle Buck, Susie Q and trucking. Our routine had completely disappeared, but I was the world's dancing fool. Boogie-woogie, the Charleston. When the band was moving into the last chorus, I was just getting warmed up.

R.L. pursued me across the floor. He finally put his arm around my shoulder again, and by brute force led me off the floor, flashing to the end.

The audience clapped and I pulled away and raced back, booming and boom-rahing. R.L. joined me and again pulled me back to the wings.

I loved it. I was a hungry person invited to a welcome table for the first time in her life.

The costume rental and transportation had diminished our take to fifteen dollars apiece. I was exhausted and had the long bus ride ahead back to the city. But all was better than well. It was supercolossal. I had broken in. I was in show business. The only way up was up.

CHAPTER 23

―――――― ⚭ ――――――

As I scrambled around the foot of the success ladder, Mother's life flowed radiant. Fluorescent-tipped waves on incoming tides. Men with exotic names, slick hair and attitudes of bored wisdom came into Vivian Baxter's large dark house, stayed awhile and went, making room for their successors.

Good-Doing David, with his silky black skin (Mother always preferred very black men, saying they were the cleanest folks in the world) and silk foulard tie, sat around the kitchen table for a few months. His eyes monitored her movements carefully, and when it was nearly too late she repaid him with a sultry look, thrown over her shoulder, and a smile that promised secret delight. Good-Doing forfeited his tenancy because of a misjudgment in logic. He thought since he was her man, it followed that she was his woman. He shouldn't have been so wrong.

One afternoon a seaman friend called her from the dock and she invited him over. They maintained a brother/sister relationship.

"John Thomas is coming," she said to me. "Please go get a couple of chickens from the kosher poultry store. Tell them to cut them up." She had pulled out the wooden bowl, and laid her diamond rings in an ashtray. "I'll whip up a few biscuits and give him some fried chicken."

I knew that although the store was only two blocks away, she would have the bread in the oven and the oil heating for the chicken before I returned.

When they said cooking, they called Vivian Baxter's middle name.

When I rushed back into the house, the smell of hot grease met me, and the mixing bowl was washed and draining on the sink. Mother was setting the table for two.

"You have to pick up the baby? Make me a little drink, honey. And see if there's bourbon. John Thomas drinks bourbon. I'll put your chicken on the back of the stove." Her smile was partly for me, partly for the coming visitor and partly for the chicken seasoned, floured and dropping into the boiling skillet.

"You know there's always some in the kitchen for 'grandma 'n de chillun'." Her favorite old-folks line slid into white-folks vulgarity of the black accent.

I answered the door for Mr. Thomas, and took his herringbone raglan coat and hat.

"Hey, baby, still growing, huh? Where your old ugly mama?" He walked down the hall laughing.

"Let him in, he may be a gambler." Mother's voice clinked like good glass from the kitchen.

Their welcoming laughter mixed as I left the house.

THE ambulance screamed as it two-wheel-turned the corner from our block. I picked Guy up, not noticing his weight, and ran to our house, where two police cars sat empty, their red eyes turning faintly in the afternoon sunlight.

For the passionate, joy and anger are experienced in equal proportions and possibly with equal anticipation. My mother's capacity to enjoy herself was vast and her rages were legendary. Mother never instigated violence, but she was known not to edge an inch out of the way of its progress. The sound of police and ambulance sirens whine through my childhood memory with dateless frequency. The red lights whirring on top of official cars and the heavy disrespectful footsteps of strange authority in our houses can be brought back clearly in my mind at a beckon.

Inside, Mother was slipping into her suede coat, a quiet smile on her face. She saw me and turned to the brace of policemen who waited for her.

"This is my daughter, Officers. That's who I was waiting for. Baby . . ." Now for the instructions that I already knew well. "Call the bail bondsman, Boyd Puccinelli. Tell him to meet me at Central Station."

I knew better than to ask what happened. I held the baby tighter.

"It's just a little business with David. Now, don't you worry. I'll be back in an hour."

She checked her make-up in her compact mirror, gave me and the baby a peck on our lips and walked down the steps with the police. Separate and dignified.

Then from the bottom: "Your dinner's in the oven. On low. Oh, and baby, clean up in the bedroom before that stuff dries, please."

There was no sign of Mr. John Thomas in the kitchen. After my son and I had eaten, and I put him down for an afternoon nap, I opened her bedroom door. One chair was on its side, but elsewhere things were in order. As I walked in, the weak winter sunshine paled over dark rust blotches on the rug and showed the lighter red splashes down the sides of the mantel.

Lukewarm soap suds are best to remove bloodstains from furniture. I had nearly finished cleaning up when Mother returned.

"Hi, baby. Any phone calls?"

"No."

"Here, leave that, I'll do the rest. Come on in the kitchen and let me tell you what happened."

Over a fresh drink she gave me what she called a "blow-by-blow" description.

"John Thomas and I were up to our elbows in fried chicken (I made a gravy longer than I been away from St. Louis for the biscuits) when Good-Doing rang the bell. I let him in and brought him back to the kitchen. He saw John Thomas and stopped shorter than a show horse. Said no, he didn't want to eat. Didn't want a drink, didn't want a chair, so I sat back down and started tending to business. Every time I looked up, I saw he was getting fuller than I was. Finally he said he wanted a few words with me and would I come to the bedroom. I told him to go on, I'd be there. I excused myself from John Thomas and went up the hall.

" 'What's that nigger doing here?' He got ugly in the face and jumped around like a tail on a kite.

"I said, 'You know John Thomas. He's my friend. He's like a brother to me.'

" 'Well, I don't like him eating here. Get him out of the house.'

"I said, 'Good-Doing, don't get it twisted. This is my house and my chicken, and he's my friend.'

"He said, 'Bitch, you supposed to be so bad. You need a good ass-kicking.' "

She looked at me, puzzlement wrinkling her pretty face.

"Baby, I swear to you, I don't know what sent him off, but before I could say anything, he reached in his pocket and pulled out a knife. You know he's got something wrong with the fingers on his left hand, so he bent his head over and was trying to open the knife with his teeth. Now, you can see by that, that he's a fool. Instead of moving away from him I just stepped over to the mantel. I put Bladie Mae in my pocket before I went up to the room. When he came up with his knife half open, I slapped him cross the face with ole Bladie.

"He jumped faster than the blood. Screamed, 'Goddammit, Bibbie, you cut me!'

"I said, 'You goddam right, and you lucky I don't shoot you on top of it.'

"He was holding his face, blood dripping down his hands on to his Hart Schaffner and Marx suit. I gave him a pillow off my bed and told him to sit down. I told him moving around makes the blood pump faster. I came back to the kitchen and told John Thomas to make himself scarce—no point in him being involved—then I called the police and the ambulance."

Mother inspected the contents of her glass, then she took my large hand in her smaller, plump one and ordered my close attention.

"Baby, Mother Dear's going to tell you something about life."

Her face was beautifully calm, all traces of violence lost.

"People will take advantage of you if you let them. Especially Negro women. Everybody, his brother and his dog, thinks he can walk a road in a colored woman's behind. But you remember this, now. Your mother raised you. You're full-grown. Let them catch it like they find it. If you haven't been trained at home to their liking tell them to get to stepping." Here a whisper of delight crawled over her face "Stepping. But not on you.

"You hear me?"

"Yes, Mother. I hear you."

THERE had been some changes at home. Baily had found his first great love. Eunice was a small, smiling brown-skinned girl who had been our classmate. They had met again, and over the protests of her family, rushed to marry. Bailey, the airy false charmer, had drifted to earth and was happy. He laughed and joked again.

They invited me to their Turk Street apartment, where large Gauguin and Van Gogh prints enlivened the walls and fresh flowers sparkled on waxed tables.

He told funny dirty stories and the three of us laughed into the cheap wine and congratulated ourselves on being smart enough to be young and intelligent. We could see the plateaus of success in our futures. Plateaus where we would wait and rest awhile before climbing higher. When he looked at my 8" by 10" professional glossies, he said I had the "biggest nose in show business" but it was prettier than Jimmy Durante's and I ought to be proud.

I tried to punch him, but he laughed and swerved out of the way.

"You'll be the tallest dancer on Broadway. Ha ha." He ran around the table escaping my outstretched hand. "You'll make a million with each leg and a zillion with your nose."

Relief made me laugh out of proportion. Later I kissed them both good night and wished I knew how to thank Eunice for helping Bailey find his sense of humor again.

I walked the dark streets toward home and shivered at Bailey's close escape. Most of his friends, funny and bright during our schooldays, now leaned in nighttime doorways, nodding as their latest shot of heroin raced in their veins. Sparkling young men who were hopes of the community had thrown themselves against the sealed doors set up by a larger community, and not only hadn't opened them, but hadn't even shaken the bolts. The potential sharp-tongued lawyer, keen-eyed scientist and cool-hand surgeon changed his mind about jimmying the locks and took to narcotics so that he could float through the key hole.

Eunice's happy love and soft laughter had come just in time. My brother was saved.

CHAPTER 24

POOLE and Rita were booked into the Champagne Supper Club. Pride made me go beserk. I quit my job. How could I exchange the glittering sequined bathing suit and purple satin tap shoes for a waitress apron and old-lady comforts? I wouldn't insult my muse, Terpsichore, by letting even the idea of the Chicken Shack enter into my thoughts.

A two-week engagement in Big Time, and I was ready.

My lights in stars, my name in lights, my name in stars.

For a few months before the opening we worked for whatever money was offered and practiced daily. R.L. showed me increasingly complicated steps. As soon as I learned, he laced them into our routines. When I had no cash, I asked Mother for a loan. I explained that I was investing my time in career preparation, and when the investment paid off she would be with me, holding hands and laughing and reaping the returns.

With characteristic talent, she enlarged my skit into a full-length revue. And she was the star. She reminded me that during the war years, when she had had lots of money and could

have afforded to sit back idle, she had studied barbering, cosme-
tology, ship-fitting, welding, tool-and-dye making, and that the
diplomas attesting to her perseverance hung on the walls of her
den. She said she had no intention of ever going to work in an
airplane factory or barber shop, but if push came to shove (she
snapped her fingers), she was qualified. She approved of sticking
to an idea until it was definitely proven bad or good.

She lent me the money, without further preachments, and
Poole and Rita continued to practice.

Although I lived and ate at home, the small savings I kept
in a jar under my bed diminished. My son always seemed to
need new clothes; on Sundays I traditionally bought fresh
flowers for the house; and then there were the tap shoes.
Rehearsing wore out more taps than dancing three times a
night in a cabaret.

I approached Bailey for a small advance. He sat, stubble-
jawed, on his corduroy sofa, and looked at the adjacent wall.

"I've put Eunice in the hospital. She's very sick."

"What's wrong with her?" I made my voice soft.

"She just had a cold. That's all." But he didn't believe that
was all.

"Well, come on. She's young. Nobody dies from a cold." If
only I could get him to look at me. I went on making a joke.
"They only wish they could."

"Yeah." He put his feet on the cluttered coffee table,
leaned back on the sofa and closed his eyes.

"Good-bye, Maya."

"Bailey, it's not that serious." He didn't try to hear me and
I could not intrude further by repeating myself.

The apartment stank of dead flowers and dirty dishes. His
voice blurred but didn't rise or fall. "I've cut out all the runs
except Los Angeles so I can be with her."

The room was oppressive as if a large hand had squeezed the gaiety out of it drop by drop and then released it to resume its former shape.

I WAS getting so I could fairly fly through the routine. My romance with R.L. was danced out in the rehearsal hall, because he made few sexual demands. I gave no arguments to his monthly requests for lovemaking. After all, he was my teacher and my transportation to Broadway. But I was grateful that they didn't come with greater frequency. An artist, I was certain, protected and preserved his instrument. Pianists, drummers, horn players, saxists all look after their instruments. As a dancer, my instrument was my body. I couldn't just allow a person, anyone, to screw my instrument.

Opening night arrived. Mother had taken a large table for her friends, and Bailey miraculously didn't have to be on the road or at the hospital. The night club, which was large and bedizened with glittering spinning lights, was full.

Excitement made me glow and the lights backstage rubbed away R.L.'s pockmarks. We looked at ourselves in the large mirror. He was absolutely dashing in his powder-blue tuxedo, and I was as glamorous as Esther Williams in my swimsuit. And could dance better, too.

The M.C. called our names, and the band swung into our introduction.

R.L. said in his slow voice, "Okay, Rita, break a leg." Show-business talk. I grinned. "You, too."

And we hit the stage.

The first moment's unreality was caused by the lights. I couldn't see the audience, and I thought about the first time when I panicked and froze to the stage. Maybe this was happening again. Maybe I had frozen, I couldn't tell if I was moving. But suddenly I heard the clap of taps breaking, exploding through the band's arrangement, and I found I was on the far side of the stage and it was time for me to break. I was dancing, my feet and body were doing the right things. With that I let go, just let the orchestra push, prod and pull me. I surrendered every memory I had to oblivion and let myself dance. Each time I danced near R.L., I laughed out loud at the perfect glory of it all. The music was my friend, my lover, my family. It was a pretty day on a San Francisco hill with just enough high to remark on details. It was my son laughing when I entered his room. Great poetry that I had memorized and recited to myself in a warm bath.

The band was playing the closing riffs and R.L. took my hand. We danced to the edge of the stage and bowed. The audience applauded moderately, except for Mother's table and a bravo from where Bailey sat near the door. I never knew whether the great disappointment came from having to stop dancing or from the fact that the audience didn't jump up, run screaming for the stage to touch my victory. But in the dressing room I began to drown in a depression sea. Neither the flowers Bailey sent nor Mother's smile saved me. Two more shows to do that night and by the last one I was questioning whether I was cut out for show biz . . . whether or not it was too coarse for my pure and delicate nature, too commercial for my artistic soul.

All the area's drunks and sporting people caught the last show and I was again intoxicated. They shouted, "Shake it, baby," "Dance, baby, dance," made noise, stumbled around from table to table, and the sense of gay activity helped Poole and Rita and the orchestra to re-create the earlier magic.

The patrons may not really have noticed the very tall, big-nosed dancing fool up there, but their vitality locked me into a love of performing that continued for many years.

Except for a few "casuals" (one-night performances in convention halls), the talent of Poole and Rita was going largely unappreciated. We refused the itinerant offers to perform at stags. I said I would never dance nude for a bunch of white men to gape at me. R.L. agreed and tried to appear possessive, but probably the larger truth was that we couldn't work up a "Beauty and Beast" routine. Neither did I have the attributes to portray Beauty, nor did he have the body to dance Beast. We would have been ludicrous.

The gigs at the Elks were bright splatches in the dull landscape. In black communities there is a counterpart to the white segregated secret society, B.P.O.E. (Benevolent and Protective Order of Elks). We call ours the Improved Benevolent and Protective Order of Elks of the World. I had been initiated into the mysterious organization as a teenager and had once won prizes in its oratorical contest, and now our dance team was hired at the hilarious and good-fun *dansants*.

The middle-aged ladies, usually stout and dressed more attractively than the women whose houses they cleaned, patted me after the shows and admired my leanness.

"Honey, you sure know how to shake that thing." A big pretty laugh. "I used to shake it like that, but them days is gone forever."

Then they would run their palms down my side.

"Bet your momma is proud of you. I bet you she is."

And she was. And I was proud of myself.

"Blue Flame" and "Caravan" were my favorite dance arrangements because R.L. laid out most of the time and I danced barefoot in little balls of blue ostrich feathers and Indian bells at my ankles. I tried to imitate Frances Nealy, a beautiful black woman who had played an Egyptian dancer in a forties technicolor movie. A few Dorothy Lamour hand movements and Ann Miller's leg kicks just added spice.

Then Cotton Candy Adams came to town.

> "Let me be your little dog
> till your big dog come
> Let me be your little dog
> till your big dog come
> And when your big dog come,
> tell him what your little dog done."

R.L.'S words stumbled when he started to tell me about his ex-girl friend and former dancer. "Oh, Rita . . . she—Candy and I—I mean, she was my old lady . . . and she, uh, left me. That is, we used to dance together. She came out here—I mean, she said if . . . When she left me . . . uh, if I . . . if she . . . ever changed her mind, she'd, uh, find me."

"Okay, R.L. She came. Are you all going back together?" I was as snappy as I thought a chorus dancer would be.

"See, Rita, she's a, uh, dancer. I mean, she's great. She used to dance with Parker and Johnson. And she's worked the Orpheum Circuit." He had stopped stuttering. "She brought her costumes. Really flash. Feather fans with rhinestones. See, most of what I taught you—I mean . . ." Shyness tripped his tongue and he began to stutter again. "Wait till you meet her. She's . . . You're going to . . . I think you'll like each other."

"Sure thing, Bozo." I had never called a living soul Bozo. "I'd be delighted to meet her."

Cotton Candy was the picture of every "Daddy's little girl." Her real hair hung down in black waves and dimples punctured her light-brown cheeks. She had a cute walk, which wavered between a wanton strut and a little-girl mince. And then she opened her mouth. "Hi, Rita. R.L. told me about you. You're a dancer."

I didn't know how to hold the shock. Her teeth were rotten and her lips refused to help mold her words. I looked at her eyes and understood. They shone feverishly, yet seemed lifeless. Cotton Candy was a user.

Certainly R.L. knew. After all, he was from Chicago. I couldn't grasp why he would want to get reconciled with her, and I knew from the enchanted way he watched her that that was exactly what he wanted.

"Yes, I'm a dancer. Are you planning to dance in San Francisco?" Might as well have it out in the open.

"Oh yes." Although R.L. was feet from her, she cuddled in his direction. "R.L. and I are going to brush up our old act and get started again." She closed her mouth and dimpled. Her eyes slowly moved to R.L. "Isn't that what you said, Boogie?"

"Yeah. Uh-huh. Yeah. We'll do all the stuff we used to do."

I had to get away immediately. "Well, good luck to you both. Break a leg." I walked away from the lovers before they could see the life leaking out of me.

At home, I paced the floors. Mother had taken my son out and Papa Ford snored in the small back bedroom. I cursed Cotton Candy for coming to San Francisco and consigned R.L. to hell for being stupid enough to take her back. My career was over before it began. My tears came hot and angry. I had dared so many things and failed. There was to be nothing left to do. I had given Curly my young love; he had gone away to marry another woman. The self-defense tactics with the lesbians had gained me a whorehouse, which I had neither the skill nor the courage to keep. I had fled to the home of my youth and had been sent away. The Army and now my dance career, the one thing I wanted beyond all others (needed, in fact) for my son but mostly for myself, had been plucked right out of my fingers. All the doors had slammed shut, and I was locked into a too-tall body, with an unpretty face, and a mind that bounced around like a ping-pong ball. I gave in to sadness because I had no choice.

A few days passed and R.L. didn't come to the house. I telephoned him. He was distracted but promised to drop by and talk about it. I waited past the afternoon hour he mentioned, and long into the night. He never came; he didn't call.

If we had had the opportunity to talk about it, laboriously and painfully, I might have been forever lost in the romance of romance lost. But with no sounding board except my own ears and honest thoughts, I had to stop weeping (it was too exhausting) and admit that Cotton Candy had dibs on him and maybe R.L. felt more loyal to her because she was a user and needed him.

There was nothing about me to bind anyone to me in sympathy. No limp, no habit, crossed eyes or attitude of helplessness. I decided I'd try to sort out my life. I tried to crush the thoughts of self-pity that needled into my brain and told myself that it was time to roll up my costumes, which would eternally have the odor of grease paint in their seams, and put away the tap shoes, which hurt my feet anyway. For, after all, only poets care about what happened to the snows of yesteryear. And I hadn't time to be a poet, I had to find a job, get my grits together and take care of my son. So much for show biz, I was off to live real life.

CHAPTER 25

———————— ⟫ ————————

A FRIEND of Mother's who had a restaurant in Stockton needed a fry cook. I packed the clothes I thought we might need and set out for the eighty-mile journey. I wasn't sure that I'd find pot in the little town, so I stashed a Prince Albert can full, and papers, in the bottom of my suitcase. I refused to cry all the way in the back seat of a Greyhound bus.

Stockton had an unusual atmosphere. Situated in the agricultural San Joaquin Valley, it had long been a center for the itinerant workers. Southerners drawn from depleted farms, Mexicans and Filipinos from their poverty-stricken countries who had raised large families on meager incomes since the early 1900s. World War II had enriched the town's blood by attracting blacks from the South to work at the local dry dock, the shipyards and defense plants in nearby Pittsburg.

When I arrived, there was Wild West rhythm in the streets. Since some of the plants were still running and the police hadn't yet cracked down on crime, prostitutes and gamblers came from San Francisco and Los Angeles on weekends to fleece the willing local yokels.

The restaurant was large, seating seventy-five, and had a steady and regular clientele. But because it was two blocks from Center Street, we got little of the sophisticated walk-in trade. My shift began at four in the afternoon, and I fried hamburgers, pork chops and eggs and ham streaks until midnight. Then, to add juice to my dry life, I would wash up, exchange the sweaty uniform for a clinging one-shoulder deal and high-heeled shoes that hurt my already swollen feet. A slow saunter to Center Street, and a perch at the crowded bar gave me a chance to watch the fascinating city folks, and at the same time haughtily explain to any man fresh enough to approach me that I worked for a living. I wasn't a whore. I told myself that the fact that I might have been mistaken for one, because of my flagrant way of dressing or clinging to a bar alone in a small town at one in the morning, was simply evidence of men trying to read a book by its cover.

Big Mary was a large-boned, rough woman from Oklahoma whose husband had died in the tomato fields surrounding Stockton. She was the neighborhood's surrogate mother. She tended children on a daily basis, but when I explained that I needed a weekly arrangement because of my hours, she agreed to let my son live in her house; I could pick him up on my day off. The blood of Indian ancestors pushed her cheekbones up so high that her eyes appeared to be closed, and her skin was the black brown of old polished wood. Mary drank once a month and other arrangements had to be made for all children on that one day. She would dress herself in a clean, loose-fitting cotton dress, and her dead husband's shoes cut out to ease the strain. Sitting at the bar, she'd pull a coffee cup from her purse and order the bartender, "Fill it up!" After drinking the contents, she'd ask the bartender to wash the cup and fill it up again. She would sit, sipping, staring straight ahead, until she had drunk three cups of bourbon. Then she would pay, and without having passed the time of day with anyone, leave the bar as straight as she had entered it.

Her way with children was to feed them well and coddle them. She fell into baby talk whenever children were mentioned, even if none were present.

Her thick Oklahoma accent slurred and her tongue protruded through the evenly shaped, full black lips. I figured that such a display of affection couldn't hurt my son, so I worked without great concern, and devoted myself to the serious business of accumulating a wardrobe.

BOYS seem to think that girls hold the keys to all happiness, because the female is supposed to have the right of consent and/or dissent. I've heard older men reflect on their youth, and an edge of hostile envy drags across their voices as they conjure up the girls who whetted but didn't satisfy their sexual appetites. It's interesting that they didn't realize in those yearning days past, nor even in the present days of understanding, that if the female had the right to decide, she suffered from her inability to instigate. That is, she could only say yes or no if she was asked.

She spends half her time making herself attractive to men, and the other half trying to divine which of the attracted are serious enough to marry her, and which wish to ram her against the nearest wall and jab into her recklessly, then leave her leaning, legs trembling, cold wet evidence running down her inner thigh. Which one will come to her again, proud to take her to his friends, and which will have friends who only know of her as the easy girl with good (or even bad) poontang?

The crushing insecurity of youth, and the built-in suspicion between the sexes, militate against the survival of the
species, and yet, men do legalize their poking, and women do
get revenge their whole lives through for the desperate days of
insecurity and bear children so that the whole process remains
in process.

Alas.

The Poole-Rita partnership, with a little romance on the
side, had left me yearning more for the stage and music and
bravos of audiences than for a lover's arms.

But as fry cook in a small restaurant in the farm community, my fantasies were little different from any other girl of
my age. He would come. He would. Just walk into my life, see
me and fall everlastingly in love. I had the affliction suffered
by most young women. The sexual excitement of my teens
had abated, and I looked forward to a husband who would
love me ethereally, spiritually, and on rare (but beautiful)
occasions, physically.

He would be a little younger than my father, and handsome in that casual way. His conservative clothes would fit
well, and he'd talk to me softly and look at me penetratingly.
He'd often pat me and tell me how proud he was of me and
I'd strain to make him even prouder. We would live quietly in
a pretty little house and I'd have another child, a girl, and the
two children (whom he'd love equally) would climb over his
knees and I would make three-layer caramel cakes in my elec-
tric kitchen until they went off to college.

L.D. Tolbrook was my father's age, my father's color, and
was as conservative as a black Episcopalian preacher. He wore
tailor-made clothes and his rare smile showed teeth so anxious
they clambered over each other. His hands were dainty and

his long brown fingers ended with natural-polish manicured
nails.

One night he was with a party who had come to the
restaurant for a midnight breakfast. I had changed into evening clothes but my replacement hadn't yet come. When the
waitress explained the situation to L.D.'s party, he came to the
door of the kitchen and said, "Excuse me. I wanted a word
with the chef." His voice was soft.

"I'm the swing-shift cook, but I'm off now." I didn't really
look at him.

"Well, I understand that." His smile came from a deep
well of understanding. "But my party is especially hungry.
And we'd take anything you'd give us." He looked at
my dress. "I'd make it worth your while to be late to your
party."

"I'm not going to a—" Before my mouth could close.

He peeled a ten-dollar bill off his money roll. "Give us
bacon and eggs, or ham and eggs. Or anything and any way
you fix them. We'll be happy."

I needed the money, so I took it and turned to go back to
the dressing room and change my clothes.

"What's your name?"

"Rita."

"All right, Miss Rita. Thank you. We all thank you." He
pushed his way through the door.

Though I prided myself on tender sensitivity, I have never
known when a great love affair was beginning. Some barri-
cade lies midway in my mind, and I'm usually on my back
scrutinizing a ceiling before it is borne in on me that this is the
man I fantasized in my late night fingering.

L.D. (Louis David) came the next night a half-hour before

midnight, had breakfast and asked for me by name. The waitress brought the message and I went out uniformed and shining with sweat.

He stood. "Miss Rita." He pulled out a chair. "Can you have a seat with me?"

I told him I was still working.

"If you're not busy after, I'd like to invite you for a ride . . . er, I guess you wouldn't want breakfast." His lips pulled back a little to let me know he'd made a joke.

"No thanks, no breakfast." And, I thought, no ride either. This dry little man couldn't compete with the bar on Center Street.

"I'll tell you how I happened to be here."

He was still standing. My eyes looked straight into his forehead where curly black hair retreated from the advance of scalp.

"After I dropped those people off last night, I went to the gambling shack. Something happened to me. I couldn't keep my mind on the game. Kept forgetting what I was doing. I kept on thinking how sweet it was of you to get out of your nice clothes and fix us something to eat."

His head dropped and his eyes lifted shyly. "I knew it wasn't for the tenner. Something about you told me that." It was time for my eyes to drop.

"So I sat around awhile, then I went on home. This afternoon I got up and went back and cleaned the house out. I won six hundred playing Koch. Then I thought I might pick up that nice lady and spend some of this money on her."

Here he pulled out a roll of money that looked the same as the one he had stripped the night before, but this time I noticed the big diamond ring and his manicured nails. I looked down and was certain the glistening pointed shoes were expensive Florsheims, and the hat lying in the next chair was a Dobbs. Here was the real thing. No loud-talking, door-popping shucker from the Center Street bar, but an established gambler who had Southern manners and city class.

"I thought we might drop in on some of my friends in Sacramento."

The glorious feeling of having caught the big one gently massaged me and diffused in my mind and body. I was lovely when I changed into something sleek and appealing, and said good night to the waitress and the relief cook.

The silver-blue Lincoln struck me as perfect for L.D. It wasn't large or brand-new, but it was rubbing-clean and shining with polish. When we drove away from the lights of Stockton, he found music on the radio and turned it down to a touching purr.

> "I want a Sunday kind of love
> A love to last past Saturday night
> I want to know it's more than
> love at first sight . . ."

HE asked if I was married. Law or common-law? I said no, neither. (I pronounced it 'n eye ther). He said almost to himself, "I must have got my lucky break. At last."

I leaned back into the real leather seat and grinned for my own enjoyment.

"I have to take care of some business. And I wanted you to come with me. I have to see a lady friend named Clara."

His words never rushed but were selected, chewed over, released into the air as if the best choice possible had been made.

For once being young was fortunate. Everyone had heard

the stories about young girls and older men. How older men were good to and generous to and crazy about young girls. I thought to myself, I'd rather be an old man's darling than a young man's slave.

"Clara is a real square shooter. Four square, Rita, like I think you are. Yes sir, honest as the day is long."

Even his idiom was old.

When we drove up to the tree-shaded house, he started to get out of the car. "Come on. I'd like you to meet Clara. She's sure to like you . . ."

I followed him.

The heavy odor of disinfectant in the house was as telltale as a red light over the door. Although memories of my San Diego experience rushed me, I kept my face straight, giving no hint that I knew where we were.

Clara was a small, well-built woman in her thirties. Her heavy make-up mask cracked into seams at her delight.

"Lou!" She backed away from the door and we were right-handed into a dully furnished living room.

L.D. said he had some business to talk over with Clara and excused himself. He offered me a drink but I explained that I didn't drink and received an approving smile for my information.

No sounds reached me from the back of the house. I began wondering: Suppose L.D. was renting a room and instead of coming back himself sent Clara to get me. If she said, "Rita, Lou wants to see you in the back," I wouldn't know how to answer. I wasn't stupid enough to say, "Please tell him that I never go to bed with a man on the first date." She'd laugh me out of the place. There was nothing for it but to submit. But submit in such a way that he'd feel badly and I'd feel nothing. That was my plan.

They were laughing as they came back into the room.

"Clara, you're still ace-high in my book," said L.D. "But we have to get a move-on."

"Aw, Lou, let's sit down for a while. Let me and Rita get acquainted." Her smile wrinkled her whole face and she looked like a rubber doll won at playland.

"This lady worked hard all night and I know she'd like to get home and rest." He looked at me. "I'm sorry. Maybe the next time I'll let you sit around talking women's talk with her. Come on, Rita, we'd better head back to Stockton."

I shook hands with Clara and said, "Thank you, I'm sure . . . See you again . . . I had a very nice time . . . 'Bye."

In the car I hastily discarded my unnecessary defense plans and tried to figure what to expect next. He probably wanted to take me to his place. But as soon as we reached the outskirts of Stockton I was going to ask to be taken home because I had a fearful headache. If he was a real gentleman, he would acquiesce.

We were as quiet on the return drive as the black trees outside the windows. The lights of the town flashed faintly and I prepared my spiel.

"Rita, I've sure appreciated you making this ride with me. I have to go to Sacramento twice a week and it's lonely at night by yourself. I knew you were tired when I asked you, but just like the other night, you showed what a big heart you had. I really appreciate it."

He swung the car into the black area.

"Where do you live?"

Again I had girded myself for no reason. "I have a room at Kathryn's."

"Cooking privileges?" He knew the place.

"Yes."

"Well, sometime maybe you'll cook me a meal. If you're not too tired."

We were in front of my door and he made no attempt to even kiss me good night.

"Good night, L.D."

"Good night, Rita. I'll see you soon."

The blue car eased down the street and I wondered if in my ignorance I had lost my chance for a life of tender loving being cared for.

The next evening when I left work he was parked outside. He flashed the lights.

"Rita. Good evening. I hope you don't mind, but I wanted to see you again."

Glorious day.

I sat back in the already familiar seat and breathed in his perfume.

"You're so young and fresh. And I sure like the way you talk. So young." He laughed a little. I couldn't remember what I'd talked about the night before, and felt the terrible burden of trying to think up something useful to entertain him.

Young talk to me was silly vacant chatter. I couldn't imagine the drivel of young girls coming out of my head and mouth, but I wanted to amuse, so I decided to tell him one story of my life.

"You know, I love to dance. I've studied since I was fourteen and I've been in show business. I was part of the Poole and Rita dance team."

We had left Stockton streetlights and were on the highway before I noticed.

"We're going down to Tulare; it's not far. Go on, tell me

about your dancing. I knew you weren't all that graceful for
nothing."

I unreeled imaginary stories of the night clubs I had
worked in and the steps I learned and my glamorous costumes. As I talked my career sparkled with success and I was a
star of the brightest magnitude, bowing and smiling to a vast
audience which would never be satisfied.

In Tulare we visited Minnie, whose house was identical
with Clara's, down to the disinfectant and artificial flowers.
Minnie lacked Clara's pixie charm and regarded me with the
hard eyes of a buyer at a horse auction.

L.D. and Minnie went into a side bedroom and stayed
only a few minutes. "Okay, Minnie, see you soon. Let's go,
Rita." He had no smile for her and no small talk. I was glad. It
was obvious that she wasn't a very nice person. (Nice persons
meaning people who tried to draw me out and who found my
stolid face and ungiving attitude charming.)

He was either running a lottery or selling the whores
dope, and the fact that he never mentioned what his "business" was told me that he thought I was square. It never
occurred to me that he might have liked that, so I decided at
just that proper time I would tell him that once I had a house
in San Diego employing two whores.

That night, I told him about my baby and that he was
three years old and how pretty and smart he was. L.D. said
nothing until we parked in front of my house.

He twisted in the dark and pulled his roll of money from a
side pocket.

"Rita, I don't want you to get me wrong. I'm not trying to
buy your affections. But you are alone and have a baby to
raise. I'd be less than a man if I didn't try to help you." He

folded a bill and pressed it into my hand. "Now, don't say any-thing. Just use it for yourself and the baby.

"All right, get out now. I won't be able to see you for a few days. There's a big game down in the city. I'll come to the restaurant as soon as I get back."

I wanted to lean over and kiss him, but his aloofness didn't encourage me.

"Good night, L.D., and good luck."

"Thank you, Rita."

I turned the lamp on in my room and looked down at the fifty-dollar bill crumpled in my palm.

It was the first time any man other than Bailey had given me money.

I bought an outfit worthy of a Hollywood siren and toys for my son.

CHAPTER 26

———— ～ ————

FOR the next three weeks I rode the California highways with L.D. I met Dimples in Fresno and Helen in Merced and Jackie and Lil in Mendota and Firebaugh, and a few women who had cabins along the road with access to the transient field workers. L.D. continued making generous gifts, saying business was good. I never asked him what business it was and he never offered any information. I didn't have to fend off his advances, since he didn't make any.

Desire for him grew in direct proportion to his indifference. I experimented with every ploy I could dream up. He had revealed to me that he didn't read books, so I tried to impress him with my great love of learning. He liked straight shooters, so one night I told him how much I cared. He had pity for me, an unmarried mother. I cried out my aching loneliness. Nothing fazed him or prodded him into taking me in his arms.

The restaurant had become a larger bore than a lifetime in the Gobi Desert, and I found no enjoyment in my books or playing with my son. All life funneled down to one smile, one man's soft, quiet "Good evening, Rita. How you doing tonight?"

"HERE'S a hundred dollars." The bills fanned out from his fingers.

"Oh, I couldn't take that much."

"I want you to go shopping and buy some different clothes. You dress too old. You ought to dress your age. You're young. Buy some low shoes and anklets. Some blouses and pretty colored skirts. And put a bow ribbon in your hair."

I hadn't worn socks in years and had hated them then. They made my already long legs look longer. But L.D. asked.

When he saw me in the schoolgirl outfit he said I was his "Bobby Sock Baby" and he was going to give me a special gift. On my next day off he took me to the city.

"This is not business this time. It's just for you. I'm going to give you what you've been wanting."

He smiled and patted my cheek and I would have thought it a privilege to die for him.

San Francisco's South of Market area was a mystery land where homeless drunks loitered before the dirty windows of liquor stores. Pawnshops' glaring signs promised to exchange money out of proportion for goods. People I knew only went South of Market to reach the S.P. railway station or to pay bills at some of the location's loan offices.

L.D. guided his car down the dark streets and I, snuggled at his side, wished the ride would never end. On the highway he had said I was the sweetest little thing he'd ever seen and praised me for wearing the high school clothes that he preferred. I was his Bobby Sock Baby, and he was going to make me so happy I'd cry.

I held precariously to the grateful tears that gathered behind my lids.

When he stopped the car and kissed me gently, long and loving, my body pressed to be rid of the prison of skin.

Skid Row's broken glass might have been rose petals, and the arid smell of secondhand alcohol was India's most hypnotizing incense.

L.D. rang the bell at a grille door and called out his name. The door opened automatically and I followed him up dim, carpeted stairs. When he nodded to me I heeled in the shadows. He walked down the hall where a light gleamed over a half door. I heard whispers, then he came back to me jangling a key. The energy of passion carried me over the room's threshold and threw me across the bed.

L.D. sat patiently beside me and spoke quietly.

"You know I'm much older than you. I'm an old man, so don't expect the same things from me that you get from your young beaus."

Beaus? R.L.? I couldn't matt my allure by telling him there were no beaus, or scream at him to undress or I'd tear his clothes in shreds. I forced my eyes closed and waited.

He kissed me and the tears I had held in the car came unfastened.

L.D. held me as if I were made of feather.

"Daddy's baby is scared, huh? Well, Daddy won't hurt his baby. Get undressed and wash up so we can lie down."

"I had a bath before we left Stockton."

He whispered, "Wash over there in that face bowl. Daddy's going to love his baby."

I SPENT the next month metamorphosizing from Miss Insecure to Bobby Sock Baby. Being loved by an older married man gave me a youth I'd never known. I giggled into my Kleenex, fluttered my eyelashes and fairly gamboled over the greensward. At midnight when I doffed the cook's apron and washed my face and arms, I flew, anklets sparking white, into the arms of my garbardined lover. We went to chicken suppers in San Francisco, where I hoped and feared the stubble-bearded gamblers in the back room would recognize me as Vivian's daughter, who made good.

The grass I'd brought from San Francisco was holding out. I disciplined myself. One joint on Sunday and one on the morning of my day off. The weed always had an intense and immediate effect. Before the cigarette was smoked down to roach length, I had to smother my giggles. Just to see the falling folds of the curtains or the sway of a chair was enough to bring me to audible laughter. After an hour the hysteria of the high would abate and I could trust myself in public.

One day off, L.D. took me and my son for a picnic in the country. He had arrived early at my house, but I got ready quickly and we went to pick up the baby.

From the car windows I watched the farm rows. They ran toward the road as if to intercept it. It amused me that the neat lines marched up and fell away, to be replaced by others which in turn were themselves replaced. They had the show business precision of a drill team on parade. The thought of cotton rows practicing routines at night when everyone was asleep tickled my funny bone. A small blob of laughter curdled in the back of my throat and rolled over my tongue. I wanted to explain the joke to L.D., but there was no time. The chuckle was out. My laughter triggered the baby's and he joined me. The whole thing was getting funnier. I tried to control myself, but each time I looked at L.D.'s disapproving face I climbed to a new height of hilarity. When he stopped the car, the contractions were beginning to ease.

We unloaded the car silently and spread a blanket I'd taken from my bed.

When we settled, he said, "You've been smoking gauge, haven't you?"

"Yes." I wasn't ashamed to admit it.

"How long have you been smoking?"

"About a year."

He took my hand and held it tightly. "Do you know that junk can kill your nature?"

I had never heard that. "No."

"Well, let me tell you something. It's gauge that's breaking up my marriage." He stroked my hand. "My silly dilly wife stopped letting me have any and she goes around laughing and giggling all the time. I've told her that I can't go on much longer. I'd hate to lose you too, Rita. Just after I've found you." I thought he was sincere and I was sorry I'd upset him.

I didn't need to think long. The pot had been important when I was alone and lonely, when my present was dull and the future uncertain. Now I had a man, who talked sweet to me, made excruciatingly good love to me, considered my baby, and was going to make me his wife.

"L.D., when you take me home, I'll throw the rest in the toilet."

He grinned and touched my face. "You're my Bobby Sock Baby. Now let's see what we have to eat."

As we picnicked he continued talking about his wife (I hadn't expected to find My Prince without encumbrances). "She's a millstone around my neck. Sometimes I stay all night in the gambling house just to keep away from her evil mind and sharp tongue."

"Why do you stay with her, L.D.?"

"She's older than I am, and she was good to me once. I never once forget a favor. Can't afford to. Now she's sickly. When I get on my feet, I'm going to send her back home to her folks." He waited a minute, then took my face in his hands. "You're such a sweet baby, Rita. Let's don't talk about it any more." I admired his restraint.

THE naturally lonely person does not look for comfort in love, but accepts the variables as due course.

I thought I was making him happy. In any case I would have done anything to win a smile or hear him laugh and pat my cheek. The job had become so very tiresome. If I didn't have to work, we could spend more time together. I loved the movies and we'd never been; also I wanted to get into a dance class so I wouldn't get rusty. I knew it was a matter of time before he'd catch on to my hints about the job and order me to quit. I would get an apartment and furnish it with the ragingly popular blond furniture. My bedroom was to tremble with pink frills and lacy ruffles. My son's would be painted yellow and white, with decals of happy animals climbing the walls, expensive toys stacked neatly in a corner, and he would sit at a cute little table learning from clever educative books. Home-baked breads would give the kitchen a solid country air, and after my family had eaten and the baby was fast asleep, I would lie on my scented bed as L.D. loved his baby in the darkness.

Three days passed and L.D. didn't come to the restaurant. I was jittery with worry. He told me where he lived when he told me how hateful and lacking in understanding his wife was, but I didn't know the telephone number. Gamblers protect themselves from borrowers by having unlisted telephones. Before and after work I walked by the gambling joints looking for his car, then past his two-story house, which sat back in a yard of tended rose bushes. Ideas of all sizes and degrees of madness plagued me. He might have had an accident, fatal. Or he might have had a heart attack. Fatal. He might have tired of me and found someone else. I hastily discarded that one. It was better to picture him in a lovely coffin, "his small face narrowed by death and his thin lips at peace."

"Baby, Daddy didn't mean to worry you." Although his face was lined with exhaustion and he hadn't shaved, he looked beautiful. He had driven up just as I walked out of the café, and told me to get in the car.

"Things have been going badly for me. Very badly."

I had no idea how a juvenile bride was to console her man. Should I pinch him and giggle or stroke him like a sister?

"I've been gambling for three days and I lost everything."

Now I could say it. "You've got *me*, L.D."

He didn't hear me.

"I lost over five thousand dollars."

I nearly screamed. There wasn't that much money anywhere except in banks. He could have bought me a house with five thousand dollars.

"And I'm up to my neck. I was trying to win enough money"—he turned away—"to divorce that old hag I'm married to and send her back to Louisiana. Then you and I could be together forever."

I knew it. He did want to marry me. I put my hand on his cheek and pulled him back to face me.

"I don't mind waiting, darling." I had to reassure him, to erase his deep worry. "As long as I know you care."

"But, you see, I may have to go away. I owe the big boys over two thousand dollars. And they don't play."

My God. The mob. I read the papers and had seen enough movies to know they'd take him for a ride and blow his brains out.

"Where would you go?" Anything but to see him killed.

"I used to work for some white folks in Shreveport. Rich ones. I telephoned them and asked for a loan. They said all right, but the wife said I'd have to come back to work for them. Old hot-tailed bitch. I know what she wants."

"What does she want?" I knew and hated her immediately.

"She nearly got me lynched. Says she's in love with me and don't care who knows it. You know how Southern women are."

I didn't know about the women, but I knew L.D. was the greatest lover in the world and if white men were as sad as I'd heard, I could believe the old bitch was in love with him.

"How old is she?"

"Be about twenty-five now, I guess. I haven't seen her for three years."

Old? I thought he had meant wrinkled, yellow-fingernailed old. Why, that bitch probably tried to make him enjoy having sex with her. She probably wriggled and moaned under him just as I did.

"You can't go back there, L.D. You might get killed."

"I've got to do something. This is the time I need a good woman." He had leaned back against the door.

"But I'm a woman, L.D."

"You're a little girl. Sweet as sugar, but a little girl. I mean somebody who can make some money, and in a hurry."

My salary was sixty a week and I paid twenty for the baby-sitter, fifteen for my room, five extra for the baby's milk and laundry. I had the right to take all my meals in the restaurant and that would save cutting into the twenty left. I had enough clothes, thanks to L.D., but what good was twenty dollars against five thousand?

"When Head Up had a little trouble with the Big Boys last month, his wife went to a house in Santa Barbara and made five hundred dollars the first week. In a month he was clear."

"Doing what?"

He still thought I was a square. "But I don't know if I could let anybody I love do that kind of business. I don't think my life is worth a nice woman, my woman, giving up that much of herself."

"L.D., if a woman loves a man, there is nothing too precious for her to sacrifice and nothing too much for him to ask." I had to make him know that I was as capable of doing him a favor as his aging wife. He said nothing.

"Love is blind and hides a multitude of faults. I know what you're talking about, and prostitution is like beauty. It is in the eye of the beholder. There are married women who are more whorish than a street prostitute because they have sold their bodies for marriage licenses, and there are some women who sleep with men for money who have great integrity because they are doing it for a purpose."

"Do you really think that, baby?" His face was beginning to look better.

"Yes, and I'd do it to help you."

He leaned forward and folded me in his arms.

"You sweet child. No, that's wrong. Sweet woman." He pulled away and saw the tears sliding down my face. "What's that for? I didn't ask you to do anything."

"No, I'm just crying out of joy. That you'll let me help you."

"I heard of women like you, but I never thought I'd have one to call my own. My own." He patted me and kissed away my tears.

"Clara. You remember Clara? I think she took to you. I would trust her with you. Clara runs a straight house. No three-way girls and no freak parties." His voice ordered angrily, "I don't want you to get in no freak parties, you understand?"

"Yes, Lou, I understand."

"When this is all over, I want us to be able to get married and I don't want you remembering nothing that I don't do to you. I always want to be able to make you happy, I want you to keep on being my little Bobby Sock Baby."

CHAPTER 27

———————————⬤———————————

"YOU sure are starting at a good time. The radio said rain today."

I sat in an uncomfortable chair and watched the two women.

Clara looked up at me and explained, "Tricks walk in the rain." She laughed. "I'm sure I don't know why. If I was them, I'd rather stay in my own bed." She laughed again. "By myself." Chuckle.

Bea's voice interrupted Clara's amusement. "Goddam. Don't say nothing like that, you'll put the bad mouth on the day. I want to be in bed with ten tricks by noon. It's already nine o'clock and I haven't even broke luck yet."

Carefully applied make-up did not disguise the woman's hard features. When I met her the night before, I had decided she wasn't nearly as nice as Clara, and although I would work with her, we'd never become friends.

"New girl gets to break luck." Clara laid on a little authority. "You know how it goes."

The language was new but its meaning was clear, and I

wanted above all things not to appear stupid and not to display my immobilizing nervousness. I tried to concentrate on what the women were doing. Their fingers darted making knots in long strings of heavy white twine.

Bea looked up at me, disdain a mist across her face. "You a cherry, ain't you?"

"Yes." Lying would get me nothing.

"Well, that's a thirty-second business. When you turn the first trick, you'll be a 'ho. A stone 'ho. I mean for life." She grinned sourer than a rotten lemon, but her make-up and jewelry and air of abandoned sex gave her a glint of glamour.

Clara wedged in a peacemaker's tone, "Well, that won't be so bad will it? I mean you're a whore."

"Hell, yes. I'm a damn good one. I'm a mud kicker. In the streets I make more money by accident than most bitches make on purpose." She rolled her head and twisted her body. "And it's more action, too. I mean the lights and tricking all night till the sun comes up."

I wondered why she left the streets.

"I just got too hot. I was getting busted two, three times a week. So my daddy brought me down to this crib. Let the heat get off. Then I'll be back switching and bitching and getting merry like Christmas."

They both stood up and shook out strings in their hands. Clara walked to the living-room door and attached two strings to tacks over the lintel. She took matches from her robe pocket and lighted the ends that swung lazily near the floor.

"You burn string in the morning for luck, Rita. When it reaches the first knot the tricks begin to walk."

Bea had left the room to place string over the other doors.

Clara went back to her uneasy chair.

"Now, Rita, let's have a little talk. You were so tired when

L.D. brought you in last night, I thought I'd wait till morning to tell you how I run this place." I pulled my attention from the little red mouths that were nibbling up the string.

"L.D. said your work name was Sugar. I think that goes with you. You so young and quiet. Now, here's how it goes. In your room you have a tablet, and when you take a trick he pays me; and after, I sign your book. If you didn't have a man of your own, I'd give you your money at the end of the day and you could leave. But what'll happen is, at the end of the week Lou will come and I'll give it to him. He'll straighten out your bills, room rent, board and liquor." She caught herself. " 'Course you don't drink and soft drinks are free. Then you get your day off and get to stay all night with your man.

"All my tricks are Mexican. They're fast but not too clean. Each girl has her own trick pan and towels. You wash them first and after. Then you take fresh water and wash yourself good. Since you're a cherry, I have to tell you Mexicans aren't built very large, but don't open your legs wide. They are tricks, not your old man, so don't try making love to them. That's why they call them tricks."

Clara's superstition about the burning string had already disenchanted me, and her conversation on deception of customers erased any respect I had for her. The only way I could be in the business was to give due service for the money paid. I decided privately that I would make each trick (each man) happy and forget the unbearable loneliness that sent him out in the rain searching for love.

"They walk in here," she continued, "and take their choice of you or Bea. L.D. said you shouldn't use make-up and ought to keep on wearing those junie flip clothes. That's all right with me. When you get regulars, Bea is not allowed to pull them, unless you're busy and they can't wait. That's the same with her steadies. Anything you want to know, ask me."

The doorbell rang.

"See, Rita! Look at the string." The red dot had reached a knot on one of the strings. "Trick time."

Bea came running into the room, and the sound of her footsteps was a little more audible than my heartbeat. The moment of truth had gotten stuck in my throat and saliva refused to go around it.

Clara went to open the door.

"Hello, Papa, come in. I've got something special for you today." She stage-whispered, "A school girl."

My God, she was lying. I was already going to be a whore. Take this man's hard-earned money, go to bed with him without love. Why add lying to it?

They came in view. Clara had her arm around the shoulders of a short little fat man who wore matching gray khaki pants and shirt. He looked Indian.

"Sugar, come over and say hello to Papa Pedro."

I walked over as if I were being introduced in my mother's living room.

"Buenos días, Señor Pedro."

His eyes left my flat chest and narrow hips. *"Oh. Hablas español?"*

My mind flinched at his use of the familiar. It should only be used between family members, close friends and lovers, according to my high school teacher.

"Sí. Y o lo puedo hablar."

"Okay, Sugar. Take him in the back and show him a good time."

Bea's voice hacked through from the corner. "Yea, Pedro.

If she don't give you enough, you can see me after. Remember the last time?"

His glance didn't stay two seconds in her direction.

Clara took us both by the hand. "Come on, you two. You're wasting time." And drew us to my bedroom door. "Get in there and have fun."

I found my voice. *"Viene con migo, señor."*

He stood in the middle of the floor, looking like a bemused Akim Tamiroff. I had to say something but didn't know how to say "take you clothes off" in Spanish, so I asked how he was. He said well. I pulled off all my clothes during the long pause and he opened his pants. Dignity rode his face bareback.

I washed him and all I remember of my first great slide down into the slimy world of mortal sin is the scratching of the man's zipper on my upper thighs.

AT sundown Bea washed her face and spent a few minutes in Clara's bedroom. She came out clicking her purse shut.

"I'm nearly shamed to show this little money to my daddy. I've spoiled that man." She looked at me, and without the cosmetic she was ten years younger. "How you feel?"

I didn't know how I felt. I said, "All right, thank you."

"Clara, you ought to get the news over to the camp. Tell them that you got a cherry. Maybe that'll stir up some tricks." She walked to the door, shaking her hips from side to side. "You won't be a cherry long, little girl. Better git it while the gittin's good. See you all in the morning." She slammed the door behind her.

Clara followed and snapped a double lock, then drew a chain across the door.

"Sugar, you better take a long bath. Put some Epsom salts in the water. Take out the soreness."

I said nothing because I thought nothing.

"Don't worry, you didn't do so good today, but then, you're just starting. I'll give you a few tips. Don't take off all your clothes. It takes too long. And remember, the men come here to trick, not to get married. Talk to them dirty but soft. And play with them."

She hmphed to herself.

"You got it easy. I was turned out with white men. They want to talk all the time. They tell you how beautiful you are and how much they love you. And wonder what you're doing being a whore all the time they're jugging in you and paying for it. Then when they get finished they got the nerve to ask you how you liked it. And talk about your freaks! White men can really think of some nasty things to do."

She started to her room and turned. "One thing I can say about my daddy"—her lips prissed and she lifted her nose and wiggled it—"he doesn't want me to do anything freakish. No matter how much money is involved. I like that." She rubbed her hands down her sides complimenting herself. "Better get your bath. Dinner'll be ready soon."

I sat thinking about the spent day. The faces, bodies and smells of the tricks made an unending paisley pattern in my mind. Except for the Tamiroffish first customer, the others had no individual characteristics. The strong Lysol washing water stung my eyes and a film of vapor coated my adenoids.

I had expected the loud screams of total orgasmic release and felt terribly inadequate when the men had finished with grunts and yanked up their pants without thanks. I decided that being black, I had a different rhythm from the Latinos and all I had to do was let myself learn their tempos.

Clara gave me salts and bath oil and I continued examining the day in fingernailfuls. I was intelligent and I was young. I could teach myself the craft and make loads of money. L.D. might be able to settle his debts before the month was up.

The woman who came in daily at five o'clock to cook reminded me of my grandmother and I had to avert my eyes when she placed dinner on the table.

I reassured myself. I was helping my man. And, after all, there was nothing wrong with sex. I had no need for shame. Society dictated that sex was only licensed by marriage documents. Well, I didn't agree with that. Society is a conglomerate of human beings, and that's just what I was. A human being.

FOR the next week I vied with Bea for the attentions of Pedros, Josés, Pablos and Ramóns. I brushed up on my Spanish and tried with little success to include *tú* in my enticing come-ons. The women's conversations interested me more than the tricks' visits. Men came to Clara's house singly, and rather than having an air of celebration, they all seemed to be ashamed of their own presence and at the same time resigned to be there. I never found one man who considered how I might or might not enjoy those three-minute sojourns in the cell-like room. And for my part, I accepted Clara's signature on my tablet as a symbol of being paid in full.

Bea made an attempt at friendliness one morning. She came into the house early and settled on a stiff chair opposite me.

"Sugar, how do you like it?"

Her voice was kinder than usual, which surprised me, and as I had no ready answer, I muttered, "Well, it's . . . a new—"

"New? Screwing ain't new, is it?" She slipped back into sarcasm easily.

"No. That's not what I meant."

"Well, don't worry about it. You'll break in."

"I won't be doing this long." I had to separate myself from the insinuation.

"Like hell. Wait till you make a nice piece of money. Then your daddy will give you a little white girl."

"A what? What would I do with a white girl?"

She laughed a tight little laugh. "Not 'a' white girl. You don't know what 'white girl' is?"

"I don't know what you mean." I was trying to withdraw.

"They call cocaine 'white girl.' Some people call horse 'white girl,' too. I don't mess with heroin, though. It makes me sick. But wait till your daddy gives you some coke. Kiss the baby!" Hugging herself, she coasted away for a second on her thought.

I wouldn't tell her that L.D. didn't even want me to smoke pot, but she seemed to pick the thought out of my mind.

"They won't let you smoke hemp, though. They say it makes a 'ho too frisky. 'Hos get their heads bad and forget about tending to business."

Clara came in bringing coffee, and Bea plunged into conversation with her.

"You know what we did last night? Daddy took me down to a gambling game in Firebaugh ... You know who I saw? ... Haven't seen that bitch in a month of Sundays ..."

I didn't know the people she was talking about and couldn't have cared less what she did the night before, but she had given me something to think about. Since she spoke from experience, she was probably right. But she was talking about pimps and I knew L.D. wasn't a pimp. He was a gambler. I couldn't allow myself to entertain corrosive thoughts. All I had to do was do my best to help him and keep my thoughts clear and unpolluted. I decided I wouldn't even mention the conversation to L.D.

In the long waits between customers, Bea and Clara talked about money, their old men, other whorehouses and their old men and travel to nearby towns and their old men. They both called their men "Daddy," and when speaking of them even when relating the beatings they had received from "Daddy," their voices tightened into lurid imitations of baby talk. Their faces softened and their lips pouted (Clara could wrinkle her nose and wiggle it like a bunny).

I wondered if prostitutes, as one, suffered from an Electra complex and were motivated by a need to have a daddy, please a daddy and finally make love to a daddy.

"My daddy said he's going to take me to Hot Springs 'for the season.' " Bea sat in her chair by the door and shook her delight.

"Daddy and I went to the Kentucky Derby last year. We had a ball." Clara began to shake her nose. "Everybody was there. I met sports from New York City and Detroit and Chicago."

"My daddy says those Eastern pimps are colder than a whore's heart in Nome. I believe him too. Look at their faces. They chilly. If they don't kill their whores, they make them wish they were dead."

"Well, my daddy didn't never hit me except when I needed it. Oh, he whip my ass then. Better believe it. But no scars. He ain't never left a scar on me."

Bea grinned as if she had outwitted the men. "They ain't crazy. They wouldn't hurt their little money-makers."

Their conversations were tightly choreographed measures,

and since I didn't know the steps, I sat on the sidelines and watched. They would hardly be interested in my dance career, or my son, or the books I'd read. And I flatly, on principle, refused to call L.D. "Daddy." I mean, I protested to myself, my father, Bailey Johnson, Sr., was in San Diego, posturing and er'rering his pretentious butt off. Daddy Clidell was my one-time stepfather, but he and Mother had signed divorce papers. Mother's men, whom I had called Daddy Jack, Uncle Bob or Hanover Daddy, came and went with such regularity that whatever name I tacked on after the paternal title escaped me after a few months. I decided I wouldn't discuss L.D. at all. They were too cynical to understand that we were in love and that after I had helped him out of trouble, after he had a divorce, we were going to be married and live in a dream house with my son and lots of flowers. I would not share my plan with hard-hearted whores.

Despite my youth and high school clothes and stilted Spanish, I wasn't popular at Clara's. The men preferred Bea. She had a swing to her hips and a knowing smile that I couldn't imitate. Then, Mexican farm workers obviously had no erotic fantasies starring black teenage girls; they came to a whorehouse for a whore, and Bea answered their needs.

"HAVE a good time, you all." Clara waved to L.D. and me from the steps. He didn't acknowledge her but I turned and waved.

In the car he wore the same sour face he'd had when he returned from talking with Clara in her bedroom. Fear that he didn't love me any more iced my bare arms. When I first moved to Clara's he had assured me, "Don't worry about going to bed with other men. It'll just make me love you more. You're doing it to help Daddy." He hugged me too. Now I remembered and supposed he had thought so at the time. But when face to face with the reality, he found me disgusting. For the first time since I went Clara's, I began to feel unclean. I was Lady Macbeth. All the waters in the world wouldn't wash away the fingerprints of the men who had mauled me. I had been stupid to let him talk me into doing something that would turn him from me. He needed love. He needed a good woman to love him, especially now while he was in trouble with the big boys. But instead of using the brain I was inordinately proud of, I had let him down. His life was so unstable (the big diamond ring and expensive car were symbols of insecurity), and when I had a chance to introduce some order into his world I had fluffed it. It was clear I'd never see him again, since waves of hate radiated from him as rhythmically as the heat trembled up from the highway. We rode in silence until we reached Stockton.

"Where do you want to go?" His question popped like a whip.

"To pick up the baby."

The steering wheel almost came off in his hand.

When he parked the car, he made no move toward getting out, so I opened my door and had to ask, "Will you take us for a ride?"

"Close the door, Rita. I better talk to you."

Now it would come. The bad words, the insults, and all rightly placed. I closed the door.

"I talked to Clara. And there wasn't hardly any money at all. I don't think you tried."

"L.D., I did. I tried with all my heart." Relief flooded my brain. If that was all he worried about.

"Clara says you sit around like a judge, never saying anything to them. And that you talk to the tricks in Spanish like a goddam schoolteacher."

"L.D., I'm sorry. I just don't know what to do. But I promise, I'll try harder. Don't be angry, Lou."

"Another thing, you haven't called me Daddy. All the— I'm supposed to be your daddy." He was fierce suddenly. "Remember that."

I said, "Yes, Daddy," and hated it. Later on I'd be able to tell him the Electra story and explain why I hated my own father, and expand my theory about prostitutes and their men. I knew he wouldn't appreciate being thought a pimp and we'd be able to lose "Daddy" from our vocabulary, unless he allowed my son the right to so address him.

"I can't take you all out today, but here, pay the woman, and here's ten dollars. You all go to a picture show, but don't keep him all night. Take him back to her and I'll come over to your place this evening."

"Yes, Lou." He wasn't angry any longer.

"Daddy?" he prompted.

"Daddy." I smiled and bided my time.

CHAPTER 28

MY baby's joy at seeing me instantly erased the odor of disinfectant that had clung to the lining of my nostrils. Clara's
house and its inhabitants and its visitors were a puff of smoke
sliding behind the farthest hill. I paid Big Mary, and gave no
answers to her blunt questions about my new job.

I gathered my son in my arms, and told Mary I'd bring
him back in the early evening.

"Ain't you got time for him to spend one night with you?
How come you all of a sudden so busy?"

I couldn't explain the tenderness of a great love. And
under no pressures could I confide to her the month I planned
to spend at Clara's. She'd simply make the common moral
judgment, totally missing the finer point of sacrifice and
purpose.

The baby, beautiful as a China doll, chattered all the way
to the movie, in the movie house and all the way back to my
room. He had picked up Big Mary's run-over-shoes accent. I
kept repeating the proper pronunciations as he dropped past
tenses and plurals. L.D. was right. I had to try harder. My son

needed to be with me. I would read to him every day and get the long-playing albums for children of "The Little Prince" and "The Ugly Duckling."

I turned down the path leading to my house, my arms numb to aching with the weight of my son.

"Homes, James."

"My name ain't no James."

"My name isn't James."

"No. Yo' name Mother."

"Your name is Mother."

"No, my name ain't no Mother."

When I tried to put him down he folded his legs up under his body and held on to my neck.

"I'm not going to leave you." His heart was thudding on my shoulder, so I carried him into the house.

"Rita." The landlord met me in the hall. "You got lots of long-distance phone calls. From San Francisco. You better call home."

I forced the baby's legs and arms from my side and put him on the floor. He set up an alarm of screaming and I stood at the pay phone waiting for someone to answer.

Papa Ford accepted my collect call. "Girl, I been trying to get you."

Maybe Mother's aim had been good to the extreme and the bail bondsman's magic wouldn't work. I would be very little help, with my own man in trouble at the same time. Of course, there was no contest. Mother came first.

"Your mother's in the hospital."

My Lord. For once she's wasn't quick enough. "For what? And how is she?" My calm voice was a lie.

"Operation. Pretty goddam serious. She keeps asking for you. You'd better come home."

I took my son back to Big Mary and told her I had to leave town for a few days. Baxters never tell family business to outsiders, so I left her with no explanation, and my son screaming his motherlessness out, shut up in a back room.

I thought about L.D., but I had no phone number for him, so I asked the landlord to tell him that I had to go to San Francisco . . . trouble in the family.

I turned my thoughts with the Greyhound, toward San Francisco.

MY mother's head dipped into the pillow like a yellow rose embedded in a pan of ice. Her forefinger stood sentinel over her red lips.

"Sh. Bailey's over there." A small figure, semaphored on a chaise longue in the corner of the hospital room.

"Eunice died today. He's completely broken up. Today is their one-year anniversary. I got a sedative for him, so he's been asleep for an hour."

Her face and voice showed the strain of worry and illness.

"How are you?"

She dismissed her illness. "Just a female operation. The things I had removed have been used and I wouldn't be needing them again." She still whispered. "I'm glad you came home, though. Bailey needs us. I don't think he'll pull through without one of us around. And I'm going to be in the hospital at least a week. Can you take off from your job?"

"Yes." Sure could.

"Try and wake Bailey up and take him to the house. Have you got somebody good taking care of the baby?"

"Yes, Mother."

"And make him something hot. He hasn't eaten all day. Remember, he's the only brother you've got."

I sat on the seat beside my only brother and gently shook him. He came out of sleep reluctantly. I called his name and he opened his eyes, sat up, looked around. His eyes found Mother, examined the room, came back to me, stunned. He couldn't grasp who he was or where he was.

"My?" His childhood name for me was nearly a cry. His eyes knew something was very wrong, but for the first seconds couldn't remember. The recall split his face open and tears poured down his cheeks.

"Oh my God, My. My. It's Eunice. They've . . . oh, My."

I took him in my arms and cradle-rocked his body. The sounds of Mother's crying mingled with his muffled moans.

"Let's go home, Bail. Let's just get to the house and we can talk. Let's go home, Bail."

He was eight years old again and trusting. His big wet black eyes looked at me wanting to believe I could do something for his grief. I knew I had no magic, when he most needed me.

"Let's go home, Bail." I could hide the shame of my inadequacy in a skillet and drown out his sobs in the rattle of pans.

We hugged Mother and they cried together for a moment, but he freed himself without my prodding and came with me to the old high-ceilinged house as obedient as a penitent child.

Grief works its way on people differently. Some sulk, or become morose, or weep and scream a vengeance at the gods. Bailey cried for two hours, unintelligible human sounds growled and gurgled from his throat. Then his face was dry. All tears wasted. And he began to talk.

He ate the food I gave him, automatically, greedily, never stopping or slowing the string of chatter that ran from his mouth.

He told me about Eunice's illness, double pneumonia and tuberculosis, the details of her treatment. The small talk of their sickroom visits. His voice didn't lower and become dramatic when he related how she began to fail. He spoke of the nurse, new on the floor, who barred his way to Eunice's room. "Mrs. Johnson? Mrs. Johnson? Oh, she died this morning. They've taken her away."

He rattled about his new tennis rackets and the better courts in San Francisco. The Southern Pacific dining cars and how hot Arizona was.

I let him talk and didn't try to answer. By morning he began to run down and finally noticed that he was repeating himself. "Oh, My, I told you about that, didn't I?" He drew words around as protection against his news. I gave him a sleeping pill.

"My, you're not leaving me, are you?"

"No."

He balled himself up in Mother's bed and was asleep in minutes.

I awakened to the splash of water and the sound of Bailey singing in the bathroom.

"Jelly, Jelly, Jelly, Jelly stays on my mi-i-nd." He could imitate the bass baritone of Billy Eckstine.

"Jelly Roll killed my pappy, and ran my mammy stone blind."

His voice rolled over joyously in waves. My instant response of elation lasted seconds. He couldn't have made such a quick adjustment. I joined Papa at the kitchen table and waited.

"Hey, Maya. Fresh coffee? Good morning, Papa Ford."

His face was no wider than my outstretched hand, and the

usual rich brown color was dusty like an old chocolate bar exposed to the light. A smile struggled free and limped across his lips.

"Boy, I sure was upset last night. I hope I didn't worry you too much. And Mom. Goddam, that was inconsiderate of me to go to her hospital room screaming and crying."

"It wasn't inconsiderate, Bail, you were upset. You went to your mother. Where else could you go?"

"Yes, but she's sick herself. And, after all, I'm a man. A man. A man takes his knocks. He doesn't go running to his mother."

He poured coffee and drank standing, refusing the chair I pulled out for him.

"Shall I make breakfast for you?" His grin was a little scary, something more than impish, and not yet satanic. "I've learned how to make Eggs Benedict." He turned to Papa.

"Papa, can you make Eggs Benedict? That's what rich white people eat."

Papa growled, "I never cooked for white folks, rich or not."

Bailey poked in the refrigerator, and took out eggs and bacon. He nearly ran to the kitchen closet and was back in a flash with pots, pans, skillets.

"I'll cook for you, Bailey." Not knowing how to console him. "I think you need turkey and ham for Eggs Benedict."

He turned on me in red anger. "Will you please leave me alone? I'm no fucking invalid. I wasn't the one who died, you know."

I liked it better when he cried. I could pet him and talk softly and feel as if I were effectively coping with his grief.

"I'm Cuban Pete." He started singing in a bad Latin accent, "Oh, I'm Cuban Pete." He Cesar Romeroed around the table, to the sink, over to the stove, his grin awful. In a few minutes he placed burned bacon, scrambled eggs and lopsided stacks of hot cakes on the table.

"Get your own silverware. I'm the chef, I'm not the waiter." He straightened up the pancakes with his hands and broke off the ragged edges, trying desperately to make them uniform.

"Sit down, I'll get your plate, Bailey."

"I'm not going to eat right now. But you all enjoy yourself. *Bon appétit*." He walked out of the kitchen. "I want to hear some music."

In moments, the sound of water splashing in the bathtub mixed with Lester Young's mellow sax reached the kitchen.

Papa Ford frowned. "He's had one bath today, ain't he? He ain't dirty enough for two baths."

"There's nothing wrong with him. He's just nervous." I slammed the sentence out, a barrier against further conversation.

In two days Bailey lost pounds from his already skinny frame and gained in degrees of deception.

Only once did we speak of Eunice.

"If I could have afforded it, I'd have taken her out of San Francisco General and put her in St. Joseph's. People lie who say you die when it's your time to die." He quoted Robert Benton, his favorite at the time. "Hate can be legislated too."

He opened his face by dint of will. "My, I want a favor."

"Anything."

"Eunice's funeral is tomorrow. After that, I never want to hear her name again." He waited.

"All right, Bailey."

"Thank you, My." He closed in upon himself and smiled the new grimace. I lost part of my brother forever.

I didn't report to Mother that the next morning he put on

fresh white tennis shorts and shirt, thick white socks and tennis shoes, and walked into the church carrying his new tennis racket.

Papa Ford frowned his disapproval. "Your brother sounds crazy to me. He said he's going to quit his job. This ain't no time to leave the road. Get his meals free. Tips. He can bring home butter and stuff, can't he? Nigger men ain't got but two outs now, as I see it. Keep on sleeping with Old Lady Southern Pacific, or start sleeping in the streets." He smirked. "And he crazy, but he ain't crazy enough for the streets. Shit. He remind me of them Jew boys. He's smart like them. But them Jew boys git some backing to open up some kind of little business. That's how they get their start. Any kind of business he try to start going to be against the law, and he have to be sharper than mosquito shit, too. Keep out of jail. He better stay on the road."

Bailey started staying out all night long, and when he came in, his eyelids were puffy and his movements slow. He walked in pushing before him an odor of unwashed clothes. His eyes were half shut on his secrets. In the afternoons Bobby Wentworth, a former schoolmate now unrecognizable in his thinness and color change, came to the house. He went into Bailey's bedroom walking like a defeated old man and closed the door.

One morning I stood in his empty room over the unmade bed and wondered how I could save my brother. If L.D. and I married soon, he would get us a house large enough for Bailey to have a room. I would nurse him back to health and buy him books and records. Maybe he'd like to go back to school and study law. With his quick brain and silver tongue, he'd be an ace criminal lawyer.

I thought of Grandmother Henderson, who prayed every tribulation into manageable size. I prayed.

Around noon Bailey came home, the unslept night dragging his shoulders down.

I faced him in the hall. "Bailey, what's the matter with Little Bobby?"

His tired face tried to shut me out. "Nothing's the matter with him. Why?"

"He's about the color of mustard and he's got so thin."

"He's just getting down to his fighting weight. Anyway, when are you going back to Stockton? How long can you take off from your job?"

I wasn't sure how much I should tell him. "I'll stay till Mother comes out of the hospital."

"Why?"

"Well, you . . . I mean, I want to be with you."

"I don't need anything. I have told you I'm not an invalid. You'd better get back to Stockton and take care of your own business." It was an order.

I wanted to be sure about his future before I left. "Papa Ford says you're going to quit your job."

"Not going to. I did."

"But what will you do? To live?"

"I'll live." He wasn't bragging, just making a statement.

"But, Bailey, it pays well, doesn't it? I mean, pretty well."

"You're not the one to talk to me about slinging hash. You might be a fry cook the rest of your life, if you're that stupid, but not me."

I refused to bear the insult. "I'm not cooking now, if you want to know. I'm working in a house on the outskirts of Sacramento."

"A what?" He sat up and leaned over to me. "Doing what?"

I knew I had gone too far. I was a boulder rolling down a steep hill and couldn't stop myself.

"What do women do in houses?" The best defense was to be uppity.

"You goddam silly ass. You silly little ass. Turning tricks, huh? My baby goddam sister."

His new temper was cold and sneering. His rages used to be full of fire and crackling; now his diction sharpened and his neck was stiff and he looked down his nose at me. "Who is the nigger?"

"Bailey, it's not like you think."

"Who is the smartass nigger who turned you out?"

"Bailey, he's in trouble and I'm just helping him for a month."

"What's his name?" Although he continued sneering he seemed to thaw a little. "Tell me his name."

"L.D. Tolbrook. And he's old."

"How old?"

"About forty-five."

"What kind of drugs has he given you?"

"You don't understand. He's even stopped me from smoking pot. He's straight and—"

"No pot? Then it's a matter of time before he gives you a noseful of cocaine."

"Bailey." I couldn't bear Bailey's thinking evil about L.D. "He's a . . . He's a gambler and he's in trouble with the big boys. So I offered to help him for a month, then we're going to be married."

He leaned into me and spoke gray steel, "You're not going to get married."

"Yes, I am. Yes . . ."

"I'll tell you what you're going to do. You are going to go to Stockton and get your baby. Then you're going to find L.D. You're going to tell him he's not to worry about the big boys any more. That he can start worrying about one little boy. Just one. And tell him how little I am. Also tell him that you are my baby goddam sister. Then you're going to get back on the bus and come home. Is that clear, Marguerite?"

I knew the old Bailey could be as violent as Mother, and this new one seemed even more lethal.

"Clear?"

"Yes." That was all I could say. When I arrived in Stockton, I could explain to L.D. that Bailey had misunderstood everything, so for a while I'd go back to San Francisco. When Bailey cooled down, I'd return to him. My absence would make him fonder and I'd have more chance to help my brother pull himself together.

Bailey gave me money for the round trip, and to pay the baby-sitter. I took the afternoon bus to Stockton.

CHAPTER 29

———————— ✍ ————————

BIG Mary's house was near the corner of a typical small-town block, and in the late-afternoon sun the clapboard cottages seemed to be dreaming. I concluded that I must have passed the house when I reached the farthest intersection. My mind was busy with other things, so when I turned and didn't see the house, I decided I was on the wrong street. Another glance at the street names on a sign post assured me that this was the street. Then where was the house? I started back. Here was the little white railroad house. Here was the house with a fenced yard. Here was . . . but it couldn't be Mary's house. The windows were boarded up and large planks had been nailed in a X across the door.

The two houses flanking Big Mary's were empty. I might have stopped breathing as I walked up and down the creaking steps and tried to peer into windows. The world had suddenly spun off its familiar axis and the rhythm of life slowed to quarter time. The streets and houses, broken toys that lay in overgrown weeds, were monotone in color like objects in an old sepia photograph.

"Who you looking for?"

I turned to face a woman on a porch across the street. Time was in such strange process that I had the opportunity to examine her in minute point. She was fat and white and wore a flowery loose housecoat. From a distance I made out her friendly countenance and the sweat that already dampened semicircles under her arms.

"My baby." But the words wouldn't come. I tried again and the words refused again. I had become paralyzed, literally struck dumb. I stared at the woman in horror.

"Come over here, lady."

She ordered and I had no resistance.

"I know you're looking for Big Mary, aren't you?"

I nodded.

"She moved three days ago. A big truck pulled up and took everything away."

She must have waited for me to question her. After seconds, she continued, "You're the mother, aren't you?"

I nodded.

"There was a big coming and going of the other parents, but I noticed you didn't come for your little boy. Mary and I haven't spoken since she called me a meddling bitch three years ago—she used foul language. But I broke the silence and asked where she was taking the boy. She said you had given him to her. Said you were too busy. I asked where she was going and she told me none of my business. But I know she's got a brother in Bakersfield."

It was a rattling tale told on a radio and I couldn't make it have to do with my life.

"If you want to call the police, come in. I'll give you some lemonade . . . while you're waiting for them."

The word "police" shook me awake. My brain moved

sluggishly. Big Mary had left with my baby and lied as well. Then she kidnapped him. If the police came, they'd question me about my job. A whore (well, I had to admit it) wasn't a fit mother and they'd take him from me and put me in jail.

"I'll call them for you." The woman turned and an oblong of perspiration was dripping down the back of her dress.

Before she reached the door, I forced my voice out. "No thank you. I know where she is, everything's all right."

"Where is she?" The woman's suspicion was nasty.

"I'm going there now. It's over on the south side. By the sloughs." I waved at her. "Thanks anyway," I said and marched down the street.

L.D.'S car was parked in front of his house. My scheme was to ring his bell and if his wife answered, tell her I was an old friend and had a message for him from a friend. I'd quickly tell him about Big Mary and the baby and he'd decide what to do. I was proud that I hadn't cried and that I wasn't afraid of his naggish wife.

A pretty, thirtyish, light-brown-skinned woman opened the door. Her long black hair curled around her shoulders, reminding me of a beige Hedy Lamarr.

"You want to see L.D.? What's your name?"

She had the same soft slur that made me love to hear L.D. talk.

"My name is Rita."

"Oh." Her lips firmed on the edges. "So you're Rita. Well, just wait a minute, I'll get Lou."

She closed the door and I waited on the landing, wondering how we'd find my baby.

"Rita." L.D. had opened the door and held it just wide

enough for me to see half of his body. "What put it in your head to come to my house?"

I whispered, "I told her I was a friend, L.D. My baby's—"

"Don't you have better sense than to come to my house?"

"I need some help, L.D. I have to talk to you."

He stepped out on the porch and pulled the door closed behind him. His face was inches from me and he spoke through uneven teeth.

"Let me pull your coat, you silly little bitch. This is my house. No 'ho goes to a man's house. You talked to my wife. No 'ho opens her mouth to speak to a man's wife." He curled his mouth and snarled, "Clara's never even met my wife and Clara's been my woman three years. You've been gone a week and you got the nerve . . . Go to your place. I'll be there when I get time."

He walked back in the house and slammed the door.

I wanted desperately to cry.

I had been stupid, again. And stupidity had led me into a trap where I had lost my baby. I tried to erase L.D. Tolbrook from my mind. Obviously he wasn't very bright. He had had a good woman who would have done anything to help him. And he was too dumb to even have the courtesy to listen to my troubles. And he had lied to me by not telling me that Clara was his woman.

Pity. That he thought outsmarting a young girl, living off the wages of women was honorable. He obviously had been doing it for years. He probably started in the South with white women, thinking that by taking their bodies and their money, he was getting revenge on the white men, who were free to insult him, ignore him and keep him at the bottom of the heap.

Clara must have wriggled her nose off in laughing at my stupidity with her "daddy." And L.D.'s wife probably bought the white piqué dress she wore with money I had made. I detested him for being a liar and a pimp, but more, I hated him for being such an idiot that he couldn't value my sterling attributes enough to keep me for himself alone.

There was no thought of the greed which coerced me to agree with L.D.'s plans in the hope that I'd win, in the end, a life of ease and romance. Like most young women, I wanted a man, any man, to give me a June Allyson screen-role life with sunken living room, and cashmere-sweater sets, and I, for one, obviously would have done anything to get that life.

I couldn't telephone Bailey or Mother. Even if they had been in the best of shape, I couldn't admit to them that out of ignorance I'd lost the baby.

As I walked, my rage at L.D. diminished and I regained some steadying peripheral vision. Had I melted down on the pavement in tears of frustration, the action would not have changed the fact that my baby was still missing. Or the fact that with this latest loss, I was shatteringly lonely for my baby and his arms hugging my neck. The weight was on me.

I decided to sleep the night in my old room and leave the next morning for Bakersfield. The idea that Big Mary might have taken him on to Oklahoma was squashed over and over in my mind like a buzzing fly.

THE small Southern California town on those midnight rides with L.D. had seemed fanciful and unreal; now from the bus windows it was drab and seemed overpopulated with mean-faced whites straight out of my Arkansas past.

A black man gave me a ride to Cottonwood Road.

"If her brother is farming, he got to be living around here somewhere. And you say you don't know his name?"

"No, but I'll find him."

He stopped his old car in front of a café that claimed, "Home Cooking."

"Well, I wish you Godspeed. Try in there. But be careful. These is some rough folks."

I thanked him and he drove away.

The young waitress shouted over the noisy jukebox and talk, "Anybody here know Mary Dawson?"

Conversation dimmed but no one answered.

She went on, "This woman's looking for her baby."

The faces became friendlier, but still there were no answers.

"Nobody knows her, honey. Try down at Buckets." She directed me to a dirt-floor joint a couple of blocks away.

Old-timey blues whined in the artificial darkness, and one stout bartender walked up and down behind the bar setting up and taking away beer bottles. Every stool was taken by men and women who laughed and talked with the easy familiarity of regulars.

"Mary Dawson? Mary Dawson." The bartender digested the name as he filed my face in his memory bank. "Naw, baby, I don't know no Mary Dawson."

"They call her Big Mary."

"Big Mary. Naw, I don't know no Big Mary."

"She's got my baby. Took him away from Stockton." I felt as if I were blowing my breath against a tornado.

His face softened as suspicion left it. "What she look like?"

"She's as tall as I. As me"—"as I" sounded too dickty—

"but bigger, and she had a brother who farms around here. They're from Oklahoma."

A little light winked in his eyes. "Does she drink?"

"Not often, but they say she drinks a lot when she does."

"In a coffee cup?" The smile was abundant.

"Yes." I wanted to hug him.

"That's old John Peterson's sister. Yeah, baby. He lives bout three miles from here."

In the past, whenever I had slipped free of Fate's pressing heel, I gave thanks. This time I promised God a regular church attendance.

"Can you direct me?"

"Aw, you can't walk it. Wait a minute."

He called to a man over at the jukebox. "Buddy."

The man turned and came over to the bar.

"Little lady, Buddy runs a cab service ... Buddy, you know where John Peterson's place is?"

Buddy nodded.

"Take her out there, will you?"

Buddy nodded again.

"He'll treat you right, little lady, good luck."

I thanked the bartender and followed Buddy to a dilapidated car. He said nothing on the ride, but my heart beat so that I wouldn't have been able to answer in any case.

He stopped the car on a lonely road surrounded by overturned farmland. A graying clapboard house set deep in a plot of muddy ground.

Buddy nodded toward the house. "That's it. You want me to come back to get you?"

I looked at the house, which seemed left alone, and thought that maybe its occupants had gone to Oklahoma. Then I noticed some movement a few hundred yards from the house. I focused on the movement, trying to determine if the action was caused by a pet or farm animal rooting in the mud.

In a second, my heart squeezed and I screamed. "My baby! That's my baby." One thought shot my legs out of the car and in two steps I was ankle-deep in muck, a new thought sluicing in my mind. Where does he think his mother is?

I picked him up and pressed him close. I felt his body throb and pound with excitement. He stiffened his arms and pushed himself away to see my face. He kissed me and then started crying. The restraint which had held through the long night and the bus trip began to disintegrate. He took a fistful of my hair and twisted and pulled, crying all the time. I couldn't untangle the hair or pull my head away. I stood holding him while he raged at being abandoned. My sobs broke free on the waves of my first guilt. I had loved him and never considered that he was an entire person. Separate from my boundaries, I had not known before that he had and would have a life beyond being my son, my pretty baby, my cute doll, my charge. In the plowed farmyard near Bakersfield, I began to understand that uniqueness of the person. He was three and I was nineteen, and never again would I think of him as a beautiful appendage of myself.

Big Mary leaned against the rickety kitchen table. "I didn't mean no harm. I just love him. I take good care of him. You know that."

Her big face crumbled like pastry dough and she trembled. "Why don't you let him stay with me awhile?"

She looked at Guy in my arms and her voice pinched into baby talk. "Pretty, don't you want to stay with Big Mary? Tell your momma you want to stay."

His arms scissored around my neck.

"I'm taking him, Mary."

She couldn't control the tears. "Can't you all stay one night—just one?"

"I have a taxi waiting." I started to the door.

"Well, wait and I'll get his things together."

"No, that's all right, we have to leave."

She made a lunge but stopped before she reached me.

"You don't hate me, do you, Rita? I pray God you don't hate me."

"I don't hate you, Mary."

"He was the prettiest of them all. And you was always going somewhere."

"I understand, Mary. Good-bye. Say good-bye, Guy."

"Good-bye."

Buddy took us to the bus station and my muddy baby and I headed for San Francisco again.

CHAPTER 30

———————— ❧ ————————

AT home, life stumbled on. Mother was again in residence. The record player spun disks ceaselessly, cooking odors wafted through every room, and ice jiggled in glasses like snow bells.

Bailey had given up his apartment and had moved his belongings back into his old room. He told Mother he was job hunting, and paid her room rent "out of savings." He now wore one-button roll suits in dun and charcoal-gray; the modified pegged pants and colorful jerkins were given away. And his smiles were less frequent and different. When Papa Ford said something too ribald or old-fashioned, Bailey seemed not to notice. He never lifted his eyes to check with me, and the teasings about my height and arrogance had stopped.

Since I was job hunting too, I asked where he was looking and for what.

"In the streets. I'm looking for a bank roll, then I'm heading for New York City."

What could he do except wait tables and sing for the family's enjoyment?

"I can use my brain. I've told you 'all knowledge is spendable currency depending upon the market.' There's money to be had, and I intend to have some."

"Bailey, you're not going to pimp, are you?"

"Let me straighten you out. Pimps are men who hate women or fear them. I respect women, and how can I fear a woman when the baddest one I've ever heard of is my mother?"

He looked at me sharply. "And let me tell you another thing, a whore is the saddest and silliest broad walking. All she hopes is to beat somebody out of something, by lying down first and getting up last."

I didn't want to be included in that company, yet I had lived at Clara's.

"I'm not talking about you. There is such a thing as a whore mentality. You can find it in a housewife who will only go to bed with her husband if he buys a new washing machine. Or a secretary who'll sleep with the boss for a raise. Hell, you're both too smart and not smart enough to be a whore. Never. But I don't want you trying it again."

He was seven inches shorter and one year older than I, but as always, he had the last and loudest word. Afterward, as I thought about him, he became even larger in my mind.

He had endured the death of his love and was still going on. Certainly he was limping and using a crutch I didn't approve of, but he hadn't atrophied. He had plans for his future. I reasoned that hard drugs might not be as bad as the people who used them. It was possible that the dirty, ragged, smelly hypes, who were so frightening and repulsive, were naturally slouchy and low-class. There were probably many people who took drugs and never lowered their living standards. I knew from experience that weed wasn't dangerous, so it could follow that heroin and cocaine were victims of rumors spread by the self-righteous. Anyway, man had always needed something to help him though this vale of tears. Fermented berries, corn, rice and potatoes. Scotch or magic mushrooms. Why not the residue of poppies?

The maids and doormen, factory workers and janitors who were able to leave their ghetto homes and rub against the cold-shouldered white world, told themselves that things were not as bad as they seemed. They smiled a dishonest acceptance at their mean servitude and on Saturday night bought the most expensive liquor to drown their lie. Others, locked in the unending maze of having to laugh without humor and scratch without agitation, foisted their hopes on the Lord. They shouted loudly on Sunday morning at His goodness and spent the afternoon preparing the starched uniforms to meet a boss's unrelenting examination. The timorous and the frightened held tightly to their palliatives. I was neither timid nor afraid.

I applied for work along Fillmore Street. Neither the local beauty shop nor record store needed a manageress. The realtor said his friend, an Oakland businessman, wanted a cool-headed person to run his restaurant. I bristled with the big-city disdain for small towns; it was generally accepted in San Francisco that Oakland was placed on the other side of the Bay Bridge to accept snide remarks from city sophisticates. But the chance to rise in the business world to manageress was too tempting to ignore. I didn't entertain the thought that I wouldn't do the job well. After all, although my experience had not included managing a restaurant, I had successfully lived through some harrowing events and considered myself mature and adult enough for responsibility.

I took the train to Oakland.

James Cain was impressed with what he thought of as my

college vocabulary, and the half-carat diamonds flashing in his two front teeth enchanted me. He didn't ask for references and offered seventy-five dollars a week and all my meals.

He was a large, gentle man who smiled a lot at life and kept all the details of his many business affairs in his head. He owned a dry cleaners, a shoe-repair shop, and next door to the restaurant, a gambling house. His clothes were tailor-made, and he wore them with a casual flair. If he had tightened his lips over the diamonds, and if he had lived in another world, he'd have passed for an erudite broker who regularly made killings on Wall Street.

"Cain's" served well-cooked Southern dishes in ample proportions and was popular with the area regulars. Cain had bought three unknown prize fighters and was pushing them toward championship. He wanted to upgrade the restaurant and extend dinner invitations to the successful white fight promoters he met at the gym.

He sat in a red leatherette booth and talked to me. "Ought to have a soup. And a salad. Ought to have a menu, too." When I went to work for him, the day's choices were printed on a child's blackboard near the door.

NECK BONES

SHORT RIBS

HOG MAWS

PORK CHOP

RED SNAPPER

As determined as I was to make good at the job, I couldn't decide what soup or salad would complement those entrées. Soup had been for me, in my Southern youth, an entrée in itself, and salad was mostly potato or slaw. I suggested bouillon. Cain smiled at the sound and told the cook to fix it.

"Tossed salad. Roquefort dressing."

Cain gave the signal to the cook.

I also told him that I had seldom seen hog maws or neck bones featured in white cafés.

The chef was told to cut down on his orders.

"They eat a lot of omelettes, and liver and bacon. I would suggest you stock Chicken à la King."

Cain's keen intelligence had won for him the position of tycoon in Oakland, and he operated on the theory of an equal distribution of labor. He left the menu design and plan to me.

Within a month customers were delivered large menus which offered, in Old English print,

Chicken à la King

Irish Stew

Veal Cutlet

T-bone Steak

Peach Cobbler-Sweet Potato Pie

Ham Hocks and Mustard Greens (a sop which was
    always sold out an hour after opening)

As dining business slackened, I had the opportunity to examine the gamblers carefully. They straggled into the restaurant during the high California mornings, well-cut pants bagging away from their knees; hand-painted silk ties undone and hanging, flapping, forgotten, down their shirt fronts. When their hands shook coffee onto the tablecloths, the waiters brought fresh coffee without condemnation.

The winners and losers looked equally disordered but were distinguishable by their company. Beggars, grifters and petty losers hung on their words, pulled chairs out for them, and shouted at slow-moving waiters for faster service.

The street women who met their men at the dining tables (Cain didn't allow hustling in the restaurant, and no women at all in the gambling room) were of particular interest to me. They came in tired, the night's glamour gone from their faces and the swing from their hips.

The men who drank whiskey for steadiness of diversion took their women's money in the open, counting it out bill by bill, then ordering a flunky to run to the liquor store and quickly bring a "taste." The women's faces surged with pride and defeat. They had proved they were successful and trustworthy whores, but they also knew the men would return to the gambling tables to chance the night's earnings, and the women would be sent home exhausted to empty beds.

A man who got his highs from heavier narcotics never treated his woman so carelessly. He would wait impatiently, drinking heavily surgared coffee. As soon as his woman passed the window, he stood up and paid the small check. The woman waited at the door and the couple walked away eagerly and together. I knew they were hurrying to the fix. I knew that the woman had already made the connection before she came to pick up her man. I knew, and could see nothing wrong. At least they were a couple and depended on each other.

Cain had little time to notice that all was not well at the restaurant, since he spent his days engrossed with his fighters. The operators of his cleaning shop and gambling house were hewing to the traditional lines, and their businesses were booming.

I had to speak to him.

"Mr. Cain, I'm afraid this month, we, er, slid back a little."

He thought. "Lost money, huh?"

"Yes. Actually, the menu doesn't seem to appeal to the regulars and there aren't enough of the others to equalize the loss of patronage."

"I see what you mean." And he did. "Let's keep it like you got it for another month. Give those backward Negroes a chance for something better."

He tucked up a large fork of greens, and crumbled corn bread in the pot liquor. "Some people don't appreciate the better things in life."

The second month showed the restaurant deeper in the red, and although I brought Guy to the restaurant daily and fed him T-bone steak while I ate veal cutlet, the chef complained that his refrigerator was jammed with spoiled food.

Mr. Cain told me not to worry. "They scared to go downtown and eat, and when I bring them the same food to their own neighborhood they won't even eat it. That's all right with me. I did my best." He told the cook to clean out the refrigerator and go back to the old menu.

"Can you drive?"

"Yes."

"I want you to take the car and pick up my boxers in the mornings. You drive them to Lake Merrit. They'll get out and run while you follow them. When they go clear around the lake, you pick them up and take them to the gym. Then you pick me up and I'll take you home, then I'll go back to the gym."

Hooray! At last! A chauffeurette.

I GUIDED the Cadillac slowly around the dark curves, and the sounds of the three men panting mixed with the soft slaps of the waves. Two boxers were large, muscular heavyweights who gave me unsmiling grunts when I picked them up at the run-down hotel. They sat like huge black monoliths in the back seat, while Billy, a cute little flyweight, joked in the front seat with me.

"Baby, I'll burn 'em up . . . with the uppercut. I'll cut their flab . . . with a little jab."

Billy reminded me of the old Bailey and I determined to see him fight.

Cain bought me a brown suede suit and a matching snap-brim hat. My shoes, gloves and purse were suede, and I knew I was as sharp as anyone had a right to be.

I sat up front with him and four other fat old men who smoked cigars and passed fistfuls of money in the glaring lights. The whoosh of sound in the auditorium, and the frenetic activity of people rising and sitting, walking, running, the faces turning like cardboard cutouts, made me think I had been stupid not to have attended a fight before.

The lights dimmed and Billy in white shorts ran down an aisle toward the arena. Another small boxer wearing black trunks kneed his way through the ropes from another aisle.

I turned to Cain, who was negotiating money business with his cronies.

"It's Billy. Why aren't you watching?"

He glanced up at the lightened square and turned back to the sheaf of money in his hands.

He mumbled, "That's just the prelims."

The referee held up both men's hands, and the gong rang. The boxers crouched with their arms tucked into their sides. They began to inch a circle on the floor leaning in and over as if they were trying to identify the different brands of after-shave lotion. Black Shorts, with a rude immediacy, thrust his left fist into Billy's ribs.

Whump.

He withdrew, and while Billy was adjusting, shot his right fist against Billy's cheek.

My scream lofted high and made no indentation on the room's boisterousness.

Billy wobbled for a second, looking for a wall or shoulder to lean against.

"Hit him, Billy." I was standing and ready to climb in the ring.

Black Shorts bounded away and then moved in close. As if responding to a public announcement, the fight fans began to give their attention to the action. Their low thunder diminished and I could hear the boxers' feet sliding across the mat. *Sh-h-h, sh-h-h-whomp.* There is no sound in the world like that of a man storing his fist in the chest of another man. Lions may roar, and coyotes howl, but the vibrations of two human beings struggling for physical superiority introduced to me a nauseating and new terror.

Whump! Whomp! Sh! Sh! Sh! Ooo!

The breath was being pounded out of Billy's little body and I knew it could have been Bailey up there dancing his waltz under the cold eyes of gamblers.

"Stop them, Cain." I turned and leaned over my boss and Billy's owner.

He regarded me as if I were a stranger just gone mad before his eyes.

"What? What? Sit down and cool off." The edges of his teeth showed and his fat face glimmered in the dark.

"Stop them, I said. That man is beating Billy to death."

"Shut up." I was embarrassing him in front of his friends. "Shut up and sit down."

"You dog. You sadistic dog freak!" The words were accented by the *whomps* and *shs* from the ring. "Freak!" I screamed it and turned to run.

Cain grabbed at my arm but I had moved away. The other men were questioning:

"What's the matter with her?"

"She go crazy or what?"

Cain ordered, "Sit down, dizzy bitch."

I was nearly out into the aisle, but I turned and straddled a patron who was by now more interested in our row than in the public contest above.

"Marquis de Sade son of a bitch." I threw my suede purse at Cain and lifted a leg over the patron, freeing myself to reach the aisle. I ran up the corridor to the front door, expecting at any moment to be caught and dragged back to be forced to watch poor little Billy be whomped to death.

I paused to catch my breath and consider the number of pursuers on my trail. The divisions between the rows were empty and the faces, which I expected to have swiveled in my departing direction, still faced forward.

I noticed that the roar was growing and from where I stood I saw the figure in white shorts fold down, knees first, to the canvas. Black Shorts' feet might have been mired in concrete, he stood so certain.

Billy's head crashed forward and the audience screamed its approval. I was right and wrong. Cain was a sadistic bastard. But he wasn't alone. All the bloodthirsty fans were sadistic, too. And so was Billy.

I walked the streets to my house and comforted myself with the knowledge that although my brother was small and agile enough to be a featherweight fighter, no one would ever sit eating hot dogs while he was beaten to death. He shadowboxed and danced down cruel streets, and his opponents made Black Shorts look less threatening than Papa Ford. I was proud that my brother was living a dangerous life and didn't bow his knee to a living soul.

I knew the job was gone, and even if an apology rectified things with Cain, I couldn't apologize. To hell with him, the job and the fighters. Hoorray for my brother.

Cain's letter the next day was as stiff as a short jab: "Rita Johnson, your services will no longer be necessary."

I was in a state again that was blood line familiar. Up a tree, out on a limb, in a pickle, in a mess but I didn't pack my bags (or leave them) and go back to Mother.

Survival was all around me but it didn't take hold. Women nearly as young as I, with flocks of children, were creating their lives daily. A few hustled (I had obviously little aptitude for that); some worked as housemaids (becoming one of a strange white family was impossible. I would keep my negative Southern exposures to whites before me like a defensive hand); some wrestled with old lady Welfare (my neck wouldn't bend for that).

While the total trust of a child can mold a parent into a new form, Guy's big smile (Mother said he laughed an awful lot for a baby) and happy disposition lost its magic to make me happy. He believed in me, but he was a child and I had lost belief in myself.

My head stayed high from habit, but my last hope was gone. Every way out of the maze had proved to be a false exit. My once lively imagination would not come up with one more fantasy. My courage was dwindling. Unfortunately, fortitude was not like the color of my skin, given to me once and mine forever. It needed to be resurrected each morning and exercised painstakingly. It also had to be fed with at least a few triumphs. My strength had fallen away from me as the pert features fade from an aging beauty. I didn't drink and had run out of pot. For the first time in my life I sat down defenseless to await life's next assault.

CHAPTER 31

I HAD often noticed Troubadour Martin at Cain's. He was extremely tall and dangerously thin. When I used to see him, he reminded me of the phrase often used to describe me, "A long drink of water." He came to my house a week after my job ran out. That was how I'd begun to think of it. His movements were slow and his speech a long time coming. We sat in my living room.

"Hello, Rita."

"Hi, Troub."

Pause.

"Heard you not working for Cain."

"No. The job ran out."

Wait.

"Well, you find anything yet?"

"No, I'm taking a rest."

Hesitation.

"Of course."

Delay.

"Maybe you can help me."

I demurred. This time I didn't intend to jump at the first persuasion. He was black and handsome, and when the light fell right across his face he looked like a thin Paul Robeson. I also knew he wasn't one of the men who sent out for drinks.

"Maybe you know I deal in clothes?"

I knew he was a gambler.

"No."

"I have a connection for ladies' dresses and suits. New." He shook his head before my question. "They're not hot. I run sort of like a catalog business. I'll tell you what I need. See, you won't have to do nothing. I'll bring the things, and ladies can come over here to try them on."

He smiled slowly, and dropped his eyes. I saw the Southern shyness of the man and knew the clothes were stolen.

"You know how you ladies are. Wouldn't like to undress unless there's another lady around."

I didn't know about that. I said nothing.

"And you don't have to sell, I'll do that. I'll give you a percentage of the money. How's that?"

There was nothing to think about. I agreed.

I'd have money coming in and my time would be my own. I could read all day, and take Guy to the park and to movies. I would have the time to teach him to read. And I'd be beholden to no one. Troubadour wasn't interested in me romantically, so I didn't have to concern myself about getting involved with him.

"All right, Troub. When do we start?"

"I'll bring some things around tonight." His words lingered in his mouth. "Uh, Rita, uh, I'm glad to be working with you. Every time I used to see you, I thought to myself, 'That's a real nice lady.' Sure did."

He left me a demure smile.

After two months my closets were filled with expensive

two- and three-piece suits. Dresses, sweaters and stockings crammed my drawers, and I spent my days reading Thomas Wolfe and going to the movies with Guy. I had cut down my visits to San Francisco. Mother's house was dim with foreboding tragedy and Bailey still hadn't got his "bankroll together." He was thinner and the new clothes didn't fit. The shirt sleeves slid down to cover half his hands, and his stomach couldn't resist the belt's descent. His color seemed to have faded and his once fast speech had slowed nearly to Troub's rhythm. For her part, Mother talked faster and popped her fingers louder, but her laughter shattered out of her mouth. Unreal.

There was no happiness in the house.

In Oakland, my fantasy settled upon becoming Mrs. Troubadour Martin. He was kind, generous and quiet, and although we made a desultory kind of love a few times, he had never asked for more. The ideal husband.

Troub was definitely strung out on heavy narcotics. Even when I smoked grass, he would take only one or two drags and let me have the rest. I had waited to see when he would try to introduce me to heroin and hadn't been quite sure how I'd respond. Order him out of my house or consider that he made enough money to be able to keep us both high for life? One hit of heroin wouldn't make me an addict. And maybe if I shot it once, he'd know I didn't disapprove and our relationship would be closer. Since he never answered my direct questions about heroin, I schemed to bring about a confrontation.

"Troubadour, I think you'll have to find someone else."

"Why, Rita?" Even shock didn't scurry across his face.

"I think you're keeping something from me. Or have an old lady. And . . . and I'm beginning to fall for you." It wasn't difficult to make myself cry. All I had to do was think about losing my soft perch, or my brother, or my mother, or old L.D. or the long-lost Curly.

"Rita, I've told you, I don't have any woman."

Tears flowed. "But you never take me with you. I'm not a girl. I want to be your woman. And share everything with you. You don't care about me."

"Yes, I do, Rita. I like you. You're just fine."

"But you don't want me, is that it?"

"No. That's not it." At least he was speaking a little faster.

"Then if you want me, stop hiding what you do. I can take it."

I dried my tears enough to look at him. His eyes squinched together and his jaws clenched. He looked straight at me. "Can you leave the baby for a while? Come for a ride with me."

Here it was. I had to leave Guy alone. Nothing ventured . . .

Troub pointed the car toward San Francisco.

"Where are we going?" I had expected he was taking me to his room, which was in Oakland near my house. He didn't answer. The Bay Bridge amber lights washed out his brown earth color and he was a cold, sallow stranger. I couldn't show panic.

"Oh, to the city, huh? That's nice." ("Did I ever tell you I have only a little while to live? I have a brain tumor and the doctors give me six months." I had planned the speech years before to be used if I encountered a rapist or murderer. "They can't operate. Too near the cerebellum.")

Troubadour stared at the streets and chose one. I was dismayed to see that we were on the waterfront. My God, he was a freak of some kind and this was going to be the last few minutes of my life. I still couldn't scream.

He stopped the car on the wharf.

"Come on, Rita."

"But where are we going?"

"I'm going to show you something."

There was an absoluteness about the way he spoke and nodded his head toward the opposite side of the street. A pale sign said "Hotel." I was glad I hadn't screamed. A hotel. Maybe his house was hot and he was bringing me to a hotel to show me the ropes. I followed him through the fog, across four sets of railroad tracks to the hotel.

He walked straight to the desk and told a chalky-white clerk. "Give me the key."

The clerk didn't hesitate and I still followed, a little shaken. Did he keep a room here to act out some extravagant fantasy?

He turned the key in a lock and I went sheeplike into the room.

My first impression was that I was in a city bus station very early in the morning. People sat and lounged on every available place. Three bodies were draped over a bed, men and women sat on the floor, backed by the wall. Two women sat in one chair and all, black and white, were dozing off or waking up or fast asleep. No one noticed our entrance.

Troubadour reached back for me in the dim lamplight.

"Come on." I reeled and tried to shake my sluggish brain awake but it couldn't compute the situation.

It seemed a slow whole minute before the scene registered. This was a hit joint for addicts. Fear flushed my face and neck and made the room tremble before me. I had been prepared to experiment with drugs, but I hadn't counted on this ugly exposure. As I watched the wretched nod and scratch, I felt my own innocence as real as a grain of sand between my teeth.

I was pure as moonlight and had only begun to live. My escapades were the fumblings of youth and to be forgiven as such.

I twisted for the door behind me and tried to snatch my hand away, but Troub held on.

"Come on. I want you to see something."

I was afraid to scream and alarm the addicts in their dreaming. If I pulled free and reached the lobby, would the desk clerk know I wasn't going to the police and allow me to go?

Troub tugged at me and we stumbled over outstretched legs toward an open bathroom door.

In the bathroom, Troub removed his jacket and gave it to me. He rolled up his shirt sleeve. Time for Troub and me moved as if we were swimming under water. He took a table-spoon from the sink and a small square of paper from his pocket.

The senses of sound, taste and touch had disappeared, but I had never seen so clearly or smelled so acutely.

The powder was dusted into the spoon and he dribbled a little water over it. He held three matches under the belly of the spoon while the mixture simmered. The sweet smell went into my nose and unlocked my tongue. "Don't do it, Troub. Please don't."

"Shut up and watch me." He tied his arm above the elbow with his tie and tightened it with his teeth. Then he took a syringe from the grimy face bowl and filled it with the hot clear liquid. High-standing keloid scars ran down his inner arm, and the black flesh was purple and yellow in a place, with fresh sores. He pushed the needle into a scar and wiggled it around, then took it out and tried another.

"Please, Troub."

"Shut up and watch this."

The needle pricked one of the soft scabs and rich yellow pus flowed out and down his arm to the wrist.

My tears, which had been terror-frozen, thawed at the sight of the man who had been so nice to me, jabbing and picking in his own flesh, oblivious to the pain and the ugliness.

The needle found its place and blood, mixed with a few drops of heroin, had snaked across his upheld arm. He loosened the tie with his teeth, and as if I had X-ray vision, I watched the narcotic reach his brain. His face muscles slackened and he leaned heavily against the wall.

"Now, you want some?" Slow lips, slow question.

"No."

"You sure? I can cook up for you." His head lolled, but he kept his eyes on me.

"I'm sure. I don't want it."

"Then I want you to promise me you won't use shit. That's why they call it shit. It is. You a nice lady, Rita. I don't want to see you change. Promise me you'll stay like I found you. Nice."

"I promise."

"Let me rest a little in the car, then I'll take you home."

He slumped behind the steering wheel for a half-hour and I watched him.

I thought about the kindness of the man. I had wanted him before for the security I thought he'd give me. I loved him as he slouched, nodding, his mouth open and the saliva sliding down his chin as slowly as the blood had flowed down his arm. No one had ever cared for me so much. He had exposed himself to me to teach me a lesson and I learned it as I sat in the dark car inhaling the odors of the wharf. The life of the underworld was truly a rat race, and most of its inhabitants scurried like rodents in the sewers and gutters of the world. I had walked the precipice and seen it all; and at the critical moment, one man's generosity pushed me safely away from the edge.

He finally awakened and we headed back to Oakland. In front of my house I told him he should take his clothes. I explained that I planned to move back to the city.

He said, "Sell them, you need the money. You've got a baby. There's plenty more stores and plenty more clothes."

The next day I took the clothes, my bags and Guy back to Mother's. I had no idea what I was going to make of my life, but I had given a promise and found my innocence. I swore I'd never lose it again.

ABOUT THE AUTHOR

MAYA ANGELOU, author of the bestselling *I Know Why the Caged Bird Sings, Gather Together in My Name, Singin' and Swingin' and Gettin' Merry Like Christmas* and *The Heart of a Woman,* has also written five collections of poetry: *Just Give Me a Cool Drink of Water 'fore I Diiie*; *Oh Pray My Wings Are Gonna Fit Me Well*; *And Still I Rise*; *Shaker, Why Don't You Sing?* and *I Shall Not Be Moved,* as well as *On the Pulse of Morning*, which was read by her at the inauguration of President William Jefferson Clinton on January 20, 1993. In theater, she produced, directed and starred in *Cabaret for Freedom* in collaboration with Godfrey Cambridge at New York's Village Gate, starred in Genet's *The Blacks* at the St. Mark's Playhouse and adapted Sophocles' *Ajax,* which premiered at the Mark Taper Forum in Los Angeles in 1974. In film and television, she wrote the original screenplay and musical score for the film *Georgia, Georgia* and wrote and produced a ten-part TV series on African traditions in American life. In the sixties, at the request of Dr. Martin Luther King, Jr., she became Northern Coordinator for the Southern Christian Leadership Conference, and in 1975 she received the *Ladies' Home Journal* Woman of the Year Award in communications. She has received numerous honorary degrees, was appointed by President Jimmy Carter to the National Commission on the Observance of International Women's Year and by President Gerald R. Ford to the American Revolution Bicentennial Advisory Council. She is on the board of trustees of the American Film Institute. One of the few female members of the Directors Guild, Angelou is the author of the television screenplays *I Know Why the Caged Bird Sings* and *The Sisters*. Most recently, she wrote the lyrics for the musical *King: Drum Major for Love* and was both host and writer for the series of documentaries *Maya Angelou's America: A Journey of the Heart*, along with Guy Johnson. Angelou is currently Reynolds Professor at Wake Forest University, Winston-Salem, North Carolina.

MAYA ANGELOU

I KNOW WHY THE CAGED BIRD SINGS

GATHER TOGETHER IN MY NAME

SINGIN' AND SWINGIN' AND GETTIN'
MERRY LIKE CHRISTMAS

THE HEART OF A WOMAN

MAYA ANGELOU: POEMS

WOULDN'T TAKE NOTHING FOR
MY JOURNEY NOW

I SHALL NOT BE MOVED

AVAILABLE FROM BANTAM BOOKS